Student Companion to

Elie
WIESEL

Recent Titles in
Student Companions to Classic Writers

Student Companion to
Elie
WIESEL

Sanford Sternlicht

Student Companions to Classic Writers

Greenwood Press
Westport, Connecticut • London

Library of Congress Cataloging-in-Publication Data

Sternlicht, Sanford V.
   Student companion to Elie Wiesel / Sanford Sternlicht.
     p. cm.—(Student companions to classic writers, ISSN 1522-7979)
   Includes bibliographical references and index.
   ISBN 0-313-32530-8 (alk. paper)
   1. Wiesel, Elie, 1928—Criticism and interpretation—Handbooks, manuals,
etc. 2. Wiesel, Elie, 1928—Examinations—Study guides. I. Title. II. Series.

PQ2683.I32Z885   2003
813'.54—dc21   2003048522

British Library Cataloguing in Publication Data is available.

Library of Congress Catalog Card Number: 2003048522
ISBN: 0-313-32530-8
ISSN: 1522-7979

First published in 2003

Greenwood Press, 88 Post Road West, Westport, CT 06881
An imprint of Greenwood Publishing Group, Inc.
www.greenwood.com

Printed in the United States of America

The paper used in this book complies with the
Permanent Paper Standard issued by the National
Information Standards Organization (Z39.48-1984).

10 9 8 7 6 5 4 3 2 1

Contents

CONTENTS

Series Foreword

This series has been designed to meet the needs of students and general readers for accessible literary criticism on the American and world writers most frequently studied and read in secondary school, community college, and four-year college classrooms. Unlike other works of literary criticism that are written for the specialist and the graduate student, or that feature a variety of reprinted scholarly essays on sometimes obscure aspects of the writer's work, the Student Companions to Classic Writers series is carefully crafted to examine each writer's major works fully and in a systematic way, at the level of the nonspecialist and general reader. The objective is to enable the reader to gain a deeper understanding of the work and to apply critical-thinking skills to the act of reading. The proven format for the volumes in this series was developed by an advisory board of teachers and librarians for a successful series published by Greenwood Press, Critical Companions to Popular Contemporary Writers. Responding to their request for easy-to-use and yet challenging literary criticism for students and adult library patrons, Greenwood Press developed a systematic format that is not intimidating but rather helps the reader to develop the ability to analyze literature.

How does this work? Each volume in the Student Companions to Classic Writers series is written by a subject specialist, an academic who understands students' needs for basic and yet challenging examination of the writer's canon. Each volume begins with a biographical chapter, drawn from published sources, biographies, and autobiographies, that relate the writer's life to his or her work. The next chapter examines the writer's literary heritage, tracing the literary influences of other writers on that writer and explaining and discussing the literary genres into which the writer's work falls. Each of the subsequent chapters examines a major work by the writer, those works most frequently read and studied by high school and college students. Depending on the writer's canon, generally between four and eight major works are examined. The discussion of each work is organized into separate sections on plot development, character development, and major themes. Literary devices and style, narrative point of view, and historical setting are also discussed in turn, if pertinent to the work. Each chapter concludes with an alternate critical perspective from which to read the work, such as psychological or feminist criticism. The critical theory is defined briefly in easy, comprehensible language for the student. Looking at the literature from the point of view of a particular critical approach will help the reader to understand and apply critical theory to the act of reading and analyzing literature.

Of particular value in each volume is the bibliography, which presents a complete bibliography of the writer's works, a selected bibliography of biographical and critical works suitable for students, and lists of reviews of each work examined in the companion. All of these texts will be helpful to readers, teachers, and librarians who would like to consult additional sources.

As a source of literary criticism for the student or for the general reader, this series will help the reader to gain understanding of the writer's work and skill in critical reading.

Acknowledgments

This book was partly inspired by an acclaimed visit to Syracuse University in 2000 by Elie Wiesel. I was privileged to attend his lecture and a small seminar he conducted on religion, morality, and ethics.

I wish to thank the following for indispensable help in researching, writing, and preparing this book: Dr. Wendy Bousfield of Bird Library; Brian Calhoun-Bryant of the Syracuse University College of Arts and Sciences Computing Services Group; Dr. Eric Holzwarth, Assistant Dean of the College of Arts and Sciences; Brittany C. Rostron, my excellent research assistant; the Syracuse University Photo and Imaging Center; and, most of all, my partner, Mary Beth Hinton, editor *extraordinaire*.

Part I

Backgrounds

1

The Life of Elie Wiesel

Up until 1944, the four hundred thousand Hungarian Jews had been safe from the mad fury of the Nazis. Hungary had been an ally of Germany in World War II. Although the German director of the Holocaust, the infamous Gestapo Colonel Adolf Eichmann, yearned to get at the Hungarian Jews and bring them also to slaughter, he was frustrated by the political situation. But as victorious Soviet troops began to approach the borders of Hungary, the German army occupied the country, and Eichmann and the SS had their chance to destroy the largest pocket of Jewish life left in German-occupied Europe. Eichmann rushed to Budapest, had all Hungarian Jews stripped of their citizenship and declared "stateless," enlisted the support of the Hungarian police, and began the rounding up of the Jewish population. The stunned Jews—children, women, and men—were herded on to railroad cars and transported to the gas chambers and ovens of Auschwitz, Poland, where most were robbed of their last possessions and their clothes and then gassed to death. Their bodies were then burned to smoke. Some healthy men and women were spared to work as slave laborers. In a few months, almost all the Jews had been "exterminated"—to use English for the German expression.

A few Hungarian Jews survived. One boy, not yet sixteen years old, who had ridden a packed cattle car to the Birkenau camp, the reception center and murder site of the Auschwitz concentration camp, began in that awful trip an epic life journey, the description of which, in fiction and in memoirs, pierced the consciousness and provoked the conscience of the entire Western World. In 1986, that boy, Eliezer Wiesel, then a fifty-eight-year-old man, was awarded the Nobel Peace Prize for his human rights activism and for his writing. He had become the searing voice of the survivors of the Holocaust. The great and overriding passion of Wiesel's life has been to remind the world of the genocidal war that the Germans under Adolf Hitler inflicted on the helpless Jewish population of Europe, a peaceful people unarmed for almost two millennia. Wiesel's humanitarian goal remains: prevent other incidents of genocide now and in the time to come.

Eliezer Wiesel was born in Sighet, Romania, on September 30, 1928 (Walker 1988, 2). Sighet, a typical small Balkan city, is in a valley in the Carpathian Mountains, in the province of Transylvania. Before the end of World War I, Transylvania had been a part of the Austro-Hungarian Empire. When Austria was defeated in the war, Romania seized the province, which had a Romanian majority. In 1940, Hungary, an Axis partner, with German support, annexed Transylvania. Up until 1944, the Jews of Sighet, inhabitants for hundreds of years, had relatively good relations with their Romanian and Hungarian neighbors. When Eliezer was born, more than one-third of the ninety thousand people of Sighet were Jewish. Most of the Jews were poor shopkeepers, artisans, and laborers. In April 1944, fifteen thousand Jews from Sighet and eighteen thousand more from outlying villages were deported to concentration camps (Fine 1982, 5). In 1945, after the defeat of the Axis powers, the region was returned to Romania, but only a handful of Jews returned to their homes. The rest were dead.

Eliezer was the third of the four children of Sarah Feig Wiesel and Shlomo Wiesel; he had two older sisters and a younger sister. Eliezer was named after his paternal grandfather, who was killed in World War I while serving in the Austrian army (Wiesel 1999, 8). Shlomo was a religious Jew, as were most of the Jews of the community. Also, as a middle-class secular person, he had respect for, and deep interest in, secular life and all aspects of Western culture. Shlomo owned a grocery store and was a community leader. In 1939, Shlomo helped Polish Jews who had fled from the German conquest, and he was put in prison for several months for his humanitarian efforts (Fine 1982, 4). Yet when he was released, he continued to aid Polish Jewish refugees (E. Stern 1982, 25). Sarah was a cultured woman, better educated than most Balkan, let alone Hasidic, women at the time. She had the equivalent of a high school education. Eliezer's maternal grandfather, Dodye Feig, a farmer, was a great storyteller who told his grandson many Hasidic folktales from centuries past.

Eliezer was a beloved child nurtured in the warm and happy home on Serpent Street in Sighet's Jewish district. He was a small, thin, dreamy, brown-eyed boy with dark hair and the side curls of the Hasidim (E. Stern 1982, 4). He loved to read.

Although he had tutoring in secular subjects in order to meet Hungarian government high school educational requirements, Eliezer's education was primarily a religious one (Wiesel 1995, 23–4). He first studied in a Jewish primary school called a Cheder. Then he learned the Torah, the Hebrew Bible, known to the gentile world as the Old Testament, and he studied the Talmud, the rabbinical commentaries on the Torah that comprise Jewish law. The Talmud is the bedrock of traditional Jewish education. Eliezer was an outstanding student: at the age of twelve, he was writing Torah and Talmud commentary. There was some tension in the Wiesel family over the question of Eliezer's education: Shlomo hoped that his only son would attend a university, earn a Doctor of Philosophy degree, and become a professor, but Sarah and her father wanted Eliezer to be a Hasid, perhaps a rabbi. Early in his life, Wiesel leaned toward Hasidism, and he clearly loved and admired the Hasidic way all his life.

Like many young people, Eliezer Wiesel had trouble deciding what he wanted to be called; that problem can be acute in a multilingual society. *Eliezer* was Wiesel's Hebrew name. His confusing birth certificate listed his first name as Lazare. His parents called him Liczu. His teachers and fellow students referred to him as Leizer. Eventually, Wiesel chose Elie—rhyming with Nelly.

Wiesel's deep immersion in Talmudic studies precluded much contact with the political world that was about to endanger his future. He was exposed to growing anti-Semitism as a young boy, but that was a long-standing and common experience for Eastern European Jews. As World War II progressed, the Jews of Sighet inevitably heard rumors of deportations of Jews to camps in Poland from Polish cities and from other countries occupied by the German army. The war had been going on for almost five years, but they were still untouched. Also, they knew that the Allies were clearly winning. The Jewish community leaders refused to recognize that the Jews of Sighet were in mortal danger. The elders of the community remembered that when the city was occupied by the Germans in World War I, the occupiers had behaved courteously (Wiesel 1995, 27); that fact lulled them into a false sense of security. In the spring of 1944, when the Hungarian police and their German supervisors came to round them up, the Jews were stunned to inaction. Some could have escaped into the mountains; the weather was good. None tried (Wiesel 1995, 63).

In one day, Elie Wiesel lost his home, community, and all sense of security. The Wiesel family and their coreligionists were shipped to Birkenau, the adjacent death camp for Auschwitz. As they were rounded up, not a single gentile, not a single friend or neighbor, came to the aid of the Jews of Sighet. Most closed their shutters on the pitiful and tragic exodus (E. Stern 1982, 54), a scene repeated almost everywhere else in Germany and German-occupied Europe. This fact has plagued Elie Wiesel for most of his life. And years later, Wiesel would learn that his beloved grandfather Dodye had his white beard cut off by laughing German soldiers just before they shot the old man in a Polish forest (E. Stern 1982, 161).

Arriving at Birkenau, Mrs. Wiesel and her youngest daughter were murdered the very first night in the gas chambers. The rest of the family became slave workers. Now Wiesel no longer had a name: he was tattooed with "A-7713" and identified as such (Walker 1998, 2). Like all survivors of the Holocaust, he would spend the rest of his life with "this reminder of German brutality," of German hospitality etched on his arm. Fortunately, the boy was able to stay with his father in the camp. That fact, luck, and a youthful determination not to give up his life were probably the reasons he survived. In early 1945, Wiesel and his father were transported to the Buchenwald concentration camp. They had to march part of the way even though Elie had had a serious operation on his foot, done without anesthetic. For days, he limped along in terrible pain, trailing blood on the snow (E. Stern 1982, 87). Father and son helped each other stay alive.

At Buchenwald, Shlomo died of dysentery and starvation shortly before the camp was liberated by the American army on April 11, 1945. He was just one of six million Jewish victims of Hitler's other war—the war against the Jews. Young Wiesel, ill and starved, was barely alive and devoid of faith. He thought he had witnessed the end of Jewish life (Estess 1980, 8). With liberation, Elie Wiesel emerged from the Kingdom of Night.

Where was the boy to go? Sighet could only be a ghostly site of continual anguish for him. He did not wish to return there and live with strangers. The city was almost entirely empty of its Jewish population. Wiesel wanted to go to Palestine to join the Jewish pioneers there. However, the British government, to its eternal shame, was indifferent to the suffering of the wretched Holocaust survivors, and it prevented Jewish immigration to the Palestine Mandate and interned again Jews who tried to get there (Wiesel 1995, 116).

Some four hundred Jewish orphans, including Wiesel, unwelcome in Eastern Europe, hated in Germany, were placed on a train bound for Belgium. As the train sped west, French General Charles de Gaulle, out of compassion for the children, had it diverted to France. At the border, French officials asked the boy if he wanted to adopt French citizenship, but Wiesel couldn't even understand the question, and so he remained stateless. Nevertheless, he was allowed to debark in France.

Under the auspices of *Oeuvre de Secours aux Enfants,* a Jewish children's aid organization, Wiesel was settled in Normandy for a while. Slowly the youth began to think that he had been spared death for a reason, and his belief in God returned to him. He knew that he had to live once more as an observant Jew.

A photo of a group of children, Wiesel among them, appeared in a magazine. Miraculously, his sister Hilda saw the photo, and Wiesel learned that she and one other sister, Bea, had not died in the camps. Elie and Hilda were shortly reunited in Paris. Later, he and Bea were reunited in Antwerp.

In Normandy, Wiesel began secondary education and rapidly learned French with the help of generous French tutors. Attempting a new language (after Yiddish, Hebrew, Hungarian, and German) occupied his tormented mind and gave structure to his life. French was Wiesel's language of freedom and literature. Throughout most of his career as an author, Wiesel has written in French, and his work has been translated into English and other languages by many translators, but especially by his wife, Marion Wiesel, an Austrian-born woman whom he met in New York City and whom he married in 1969. For Wiesel, Yiddish and Hebrew were and still are the languages of sorrow. Hungarian and German were the languages of murderous oppression. English became his language of opportunity.

Soon Wiesel moved to Paris. He had almost no money. He was hungry all the time because he could only afford one meal a day. Officially unable to work because he was stateless, he received charity and earned a little money privately teaching the Talmud and as a Hebrew instructor.

In 1948, Wiesel, hungry for knowledge and because as a registered student he would be permitted to work, began to take courses at the Sorbonne where he studied philosophy, literature, and psychology (Wiesel 1995, 154–55). He was trying to understand and find some philosophical meaning in what had happened to the Jewish people, to his family, and to himself. He confronted the age-old question of theodicy: how can God's justice be validated in the face of all the evil the Deity allows to exist?

Also in 1948, when the new State of Israel, which had come into existence by the actions of the United Nations, was immediately attacked by its Arab neighbors and had to fight for its life, Wiesel went to an Israeli recruiting office in Paris to volunteer to fight for the Jewish homeland. The examining physician sent him away, advising medical treatment instead of combat (E. Stern 1982, 124–25). The next year, with the Israeli War of Independence still in progress, Wiesel made it to Israel as the Paris correspondent for an Israeli newspaper. His urge to walk in Jerusalem was finally satisfied.

Wiesel's studies at the Sorbonne lasted four years, without completion. During this period, Wiesel was greatly influenced by existentialism, a philosophy that developed out of the suffering, despair, and deep residual depression that engulfed Western thinkers as they contemplated a ruined Europe. Many French and some German intellectuals came to believe that human knowledge was pitifully limited and totally bound to sensory experience; humans were unable, considering the empirical evidence of the savagery of two world wars, to know if God existed. Yet, existentialists argue that a person has free will, and that each is responsible for his or her actions even though no one knows the ultimate consequence of any action.

The Frenchman Jean-Paul Sartre and the German Martin Heidegger were convinced that because God does not exist and because life ends in nothingness, there was no condition possible for humans but anguish and despair. Perhaps the concentration camp was a perfect metaphor for twentieth-century existence: The world is a prison. After we have suffered, our bodies will be destroyed. That we are suffering is the only proof that we are living. Another French existentialist, Albert Camus, saw life as essentially absurd. How else could one account for the insanity of the twentieth century?

In another French thinker, André Malraux, however, Wiesel found some hope to cling to. There was, after all, art, literature, and music; these are long-lived, and they elevate us. War, disease, famine, and tyranny were not humanity's only products. And the Jewish philosopher Martin Buber showed Wiesel how the study of his own Hasidic tradition, with its concept of religious faith as a dialogue between an individual person and God, what Buber called an I-Thou relationship, could coexist with the empiricism of existentialism (Wiesel 1995, 154–55).

However, it was the French Roman Catholic novelist and moral philosopher François Mauriac who had the greatest influence on young Wiesel (Walker 1988, 4). Their first meeting, when Wiesel interviewed Mauriac for an Israeli newspaper, was combative. It was 1954, and Mauriac had been awarded the Nobel Prize in literature only two years before. Mauriac began to talk about how much Christians and Jews had in common. He then talked of the sufferings of Christ on the cross. Wiesel was infuriated: he informed Mauriac that only ten years before, so many Jewish children had suffered infinitely more than Jesus, but no one spoke of them (Estess 1980, 12). Mauriac's response was simply that Wiesel himself must speak out. He had a responsibility to share his concentration camp experiences with the world. It was wrong of him to have remained silent all this time.

The Roman Catholic moralist, who had served in the French Resistance during the German occupation, and the Holocaust survivor became friends. And Wiesel began to write about the Holocaust.

Initially, Wiesel wrote a straightforward, 800-page memoir, in Yiddish, of his experience in the concentration camps. It was published by the Jewish community in Buenos Aires in 1956 under the title *Un di Velt Hot Geshvign,* translated as *And the World Remained Silent.* He wrote it in Yiddish perhaps because he thought that only Jewish people would be interested in his story. Most Holocaust survivors, most Jews, and, indeed, most people in the world wanted to forget about the Holocaust; it was just too great a nightmare to cope with. It implied terrible things about the capacity of educated, cultured people to be so completely evil. It was as if humanity had a psychopathic relative in the attic that it had to keep out of sight and mind.

In 1958, encouraged again by his mentor, François Mauriac, Wiesel shortened and translated the text into French, the language he would use for most of his writing. *La Nuit* is only 127 pages long, and it has a preface by Mauriac, who also helped Wiesel find a French publisher. In 1960, the English translation, *Night,* appeared. This book is the foundation of almost all of Wiesel's writing. From that point on, the major work of Wiesel's life would be literature.

Meanwhile, Wiesel had found a temporary calling in journalism, writing for French, Jewish, and—after learning English—U.S. publications (Wiesel 1995, 158). He spent a year in India hoping to find, through comparative philosophy, a purpose for human suffering, but the appalling conditions he saw in Asia voided his hope that he could find answers to his deep questions in the wisdom of the East.

Wiesel came to New York City in 1956 to write about the United Nations for an Israeli newspaper, when he was severely hurt when struck by a taxi (Wiesel 1995, 293-99). After hospitalization he wrote for the most important Yiddish-language newspaper in the United States, the *Jewish Daily Forward.* At that time, Wiesel sensed that he had truly found a new home in the United States. He felt he was no longer stateless, no longer a Wandering Jew. Elie Wiesel became a U.S. citizen in 1963. Wiesel had contemplated Israeli citizenship earlier, but when he realized that his life's mission was to stand as a witness to the genocide of European Jewry, he recognized that the last place in the world that needed his testimony was the State of Israel, with its tens of thousands of Holocaust survivors.

Wiesel followed *Night* with three short novels about the fate of Holocaust survivors like himself—lost, haunted wanderers: *L'Aube,* translated as *Dawn* (1961); *Le Jour,* translated as *The Accident* (1962); and *La Ville de la chance,* translated as *The Town beyond the Wall* (1964). These works evoke a sense of the legend of the Wandering Jew, in this case carrying in his bundle the terrible memory of the concentration camps and the death of millions of his coreligionists.

In 1960, Wiesel had the opportunity to report in Jerusalem on the trial of Adolf Eichmann, the chief architect of the attempted extermination of all European Jewry (Wiesel 1995, 347-49). Watching the mass murderer at the trial, Wiesel, like many others, was profoundly disturbed by the fact that this dull and ordinary person had been able to commit such a heinous crime and have so many victims, including Wiesel's father, mother, and younger sister. Eichmann represented "the banality of evil," as the Jewish philosopher Hannah Arendt famously observed.

Wiesel's heart had been full of hate for Germany from the time he was freed from Buchenwald in 1945. In 1962, he returned to Germany. He saw that the Germans did not want to be reminded of what they did; it was the Holocaust survivors who carried the burden of memory in their souls. But, most important for Wiesel, he realized that he no longer hated the German people. Hatred could provide no vindication for victims, only more pain.

In 1964, twenty years after he was torn from Sighet, he visited the place of his birth (Wiesel, 1995 357–60). That experience is explored in *Le Chant des morts*, translated as *Legends of Our Time* (1968b), a collection of stories, essays, and memories. A second collection, *Entre deux soleils*, translated as *One Generation After* (1970), also discusses his return to Sighet. In Sighet, Wiesel found that although his house, street, and city were unchanged, not a single person recognized or remembered him; he left in twenty-four hours. In his third collection of short works, *Un Juif, aujourd'hui*, translated as *A Jew Today* (1978), Wiesel turned his attention to the sufferings of poor and enslaved people in the wider world.

Wiesel visited the Soviet Union in 1965. Speaking to hundreds of Russian Jews in five cities, he saw how widespread anti-Semitism was in the Soviet Union, and how many Jews there desperately desired to get away from the cruel and repressive regime. *The Jews of Silence*, first written in Hebrew, was published in 1966. In it, Wiesel expresses his sadness that Soviet Jews cannot speak out, but he is more appalled that Jews elsewhere have been silent in the face of the suffering of their Russian coreligionists. Fortunately, with the thawing of the cold war in the 1980s, hundreds of thousands of Jews were finally able to flee the Soviet Union for freedom in the United States and Israel. In the year that *The Jews of Silence* appeared, Wiesel returned to the Soviet Union, and to his surprise, he saw that his writings had begun to lift the spirits of many Jews.

A novel about new beginnings, *Les Portes de la forêt*, in English *The Gates of the Forest*, came out in 1966. The next year, Wiesel returned to Israel when the Six-Day War broke out and the Zionist State fought for its life against Egypt, Syria, and Jordan (Wiesel 1995, 383–94). Once more the Jewish people were saved, but this time they did it themselves. After having been denied access by the Jordanians for nineteen years, Jews could once more pray at the Western Wall of the ancient Temple. The stunning Israeli victory was a turning point in Jewish history, and Wiesel wrote the novel *Le Mendiant de Jerusalem*, translated as *A Beggar in Jerusalem* (1968), on the return of full Jewish sovereignty to the Holy City after almost two thousand years. The powerful book was awarded the *Prix Médicis* in France.

In 1969, in Jerusalem, Wiesel married Marion Erster Rose, who became his translator (Wiesel 1999, 4–12). Marion, previously married, brought her daughter, Jennifer, into the household, and in 1972, the couple's son, Shlomo Elisha Wiesel, was born. Now Elie's father would be remembered. Beginning in the 1970s, Wiesel began to teach in the university, first at City College, New York, as Distinguished Professor of Judaic Literature from 1972 to 1976, and at Boston University from 1976 to the present as Andrew Mellon Professor in the Humanities.

The novel *Le Serment de Kolvillàg,* translated as *The Oath* (1973), marks a departure for Wiesel in that his protagonist is not a Holocaust survivor but the child of one. Still, a pogrom is central to the plot; *pogrom* is the Russian word for "disaster," used worldwide to signify an organized massacre of Jews. The theme of Soviet anti-Semitism structures the novel *Le Testament d'un poète juif assassiné* (The testament of an assassinated Jewish poet), translated as *The Testament* (1981). *L'Oublié,* translated as *The Forgotten* (1992), has an old Holocaust survivor losing his memory, and his son substituting his own memory for his father's. The novel thematically exposes the ambiguous morality and efficacy in the use of violence in so-called good causes. Assassination, even when it appears righteous, can torment the executor for life. In *Le Cinquième Fils,* translated as *The Fifth Son* (1985), Wiesel presents the story of a son of Holocaust survivors trying to assuage his own psychological pain in his effort to learn his parents' story. As always in Wiesel's writings, the questions are more important than the answers. Indeed, often there are no answers. *Le Crépuscule, au loin,* translated as *Twilight* (1988), uses an insane asylum as a metaphor for the world of the twentieth century. Wiesel's latest novel, *The Judges,* was published in 2002.

Wiesel's fascination with and love for Hasidism have resulted in several seminal nonfiction works in his canon. Major studies include *Célébration hassidique: Portraits et légendes,* translated as *Souls on Fire: Portraits and Legends of Hasidic Masters* (1972b); *Four Hasidic Masters and Their Struggle against Melancholy* (1978a); and *Somewhere a Master* (1982).

Of course, the Bible informs a body of Wiesel's nonfiction as the religious author discusses the relevance of the Holy Book to modern life. The major biblical studies are: *Célébration biblique: Portraits et légendes,* translated as *Messengers of God: Biblical Portraits and Legends* (1972); *Images from the Bible* (1980); *Five Biblical Portraits* (1981a); and *Sages and Dreamers* (1991).

In the summer of 1979, Wiesel led President Carter's Commission on the Holocaust to the site of the Treblinka concentration camp, where eight hundred thousand Jews had been murdered, and then to Birkenau/Auschwitz. Wiesel and other survivors stood in the ruins of the gas chambers and recited the most important of all Jewish prayers: the Shema Yisrael, "Hear, O Israel, the Lord our God, the Lord is One."

Elie Wiesel has been a social activist as well as a person of letters. In February 1980, for example, he joined a group of humanitarians from all over the world and traveled to the Thai-Cambodian border to try to take twenty truckloads of food and medicine into Cambodia. In 1985, in recognition of his work as chairperson of the United States Holocaust Memorial Council, his efforts in advancing human rights, and his literary successes, Wiesel received the Congressional Gold Medal for Achievement from President Ronald Reagan. Honorary degrees began to pile up even before Wiesel received the Nobel Peace Prize (Wiesel 1999, 253-74). To date, he has received over eighty honorary doctorates and innumerable other awards for his humanitarian efforts and for his writing.

On July 29, 2002, Elie Wiesel returned once more to Sighet, the town from which he and his family were deported to Auschwitz. This time he was accompanied by Ion Iliescu, president of Romania. There Wiesel called on the Romanian people to stop immortalizing the memory of anti-Semitic leaders who were responsible for the murder of thousands of Jews in World War II.

Jewishness is the very core of Elie Wiesel's being. It contains his way of seeing the world: sadly, ironically, and always historically. He has a developed sense of being part of a people with a deep memory; a unique people, who rise and fall in the seasons of history, but who always come back to life. He knows that like all living Jews, he is a Jew because many generations of his ancestors chose to remain Jewish regardless of the consequences. He is part of a vast extended family, the Jewish people.

This author met Elie Wiesel recently, and heard him lecture. Elie Wiesel is not without hope for humankind. Wiesel is a short, slender, soft-spoken but passionate man with thinning black hair. His face is gaunt and sad-looking; his eyes are deep set and sorrowful—the eyes of one who has seen what he did not want to see, and who, like Coleridge's Ancient Mariner, must tell his story. It is important for the world that his story not be forgotten.

2

Elie Wiesel's Literary Heritage and Background: Hasidism, the Holocaust, the Great Jewish Books, and the Western Literary Tradition

HASIDISM

An understanding of Hasidism is important to the study of the fiction and nonfiction of Elie Wiesel, because Wiesel's basic religious education was Hasidic, he has lived for many years close to Hasidic communities, a great many of his works have Hasidic characters or are about great Hasidic rabbis, and he has an abiding affection for the Hasids. Wiesel's vision is religious. Although he is questioning and often defiant, his religious vision "is like Hasidism" (Estess 1980, 110). One of Elie Wiesel's literary and theological achievements is his informing the wider world about Hasidism, the religious bedrock—possibly the sustainer—of his life. For Wiesel, Hasidism is not irrelevant to life today. Rather, it offers a workable modus operandi—perhaps one of several in the pantheon of world religions—for joyful existence in a perplexing world. Hasidism is a social as well as a religious movement. It is about community as well as belief. It does not engage great philosophical and theological conundrums, but unquestioningly accepts the existence of—as well as the ability of a person to deal directly with—the Deity.

Hasid means "pious." The Hasids live strictly according to the Ten Commandments and all Jewish law, but they celebrate God, who is everywhere, in singing, dancing (men with men, and women with women), drinking, feasting, praying, of course, and making and loving children. Laughter, simple pleasures, and unquestioning fealty to a brilliant, revered, leading rabbi, called the Rebbe, ease the inherent and unavoidable suffering in life. Worship of God is more than a duty; it is a passionate pleasure.

Other peoples can best envision Hasidism as a mystical, revivalist movement. It was established by Rabbi Israel ben Eliezer (Wiesel's Hebrew first name), called by his devotees the Baal Shem Tov, the Master of the Good Name. Wiesel points out in *Souls on Fire: Portraits and Legends of Hasidic Masters* that the Baal Shem Tov established the tenets of Hasidism: fervent waiting, longing for redemption, the linking of individuals with the Creator, the importance of ordinary words, and "the accent on fervor" (1972b, 5).

The Baal Shem Tov was born about 1700 in Okop, a shtetl (rural village or small town) in the Poldolia, a district in the Carpathian Mountains, in what is now Ukraine. In his thirties, after a long study of the Kabbalah, the medieval books of Jewish mysticism, he strove to bring spirituality back to Judaism when the religion seemed to him to have stalled and turned stale in talmudic hermeneutics. For the Baal Shem Tov, God was not only in the synagogue or study hall, but in all of creation. Carefully pronounced and deeply felt prayer was the way to reach God. Mitzvahs, good deeds, helped, as did Torah study. This religious turn of direction felt very comfortable to vast numbers of Eastern European Jews after a century of pogroms and declining status; it even made them feel a little happier in their long exile in Poland and the Russian Empire. For Wiesel, Hasidism is a "movement against despair" (1978a, 95).

After the Baal Shem Tov's death in 1760, the Hasidic movement came into conflict with the Haskalah, the Jewish Enlightenment, which strove to secularize and modernize Judaism by encouraging modern Hebrew literature, the study of foreign languages, and full Jewish integration into the contemporary cultural and political European world. Unlike the supporters of the Haskalah, who wanted to tear down the ghetto walls, the Hasids were convinced, and still maintain, that their separation from other Jews and the gentile world guarantees their survival as a community.

Today the several Hasidic sects are generally located in Brooklyn and in Jerusalem. The Rebbes rule over their synagogues, courts, and yeshivas. The Hasidic movement continues to grow and prosper.

THE HOLOCAUST

The most significant and most terrible event in Wiesel's life was the Holocaust. That word needs an etymological explanation. It is from Greek: *holo-* is a prefix meaning "whole" or "entire," and *kaustikos* means "burning." Together: total destruction by fire, or a sacrifice such as a burnt offering. The Hebrew word for the Holocaust is *Shoah*. "The Holocaust" per se in the 1940s came to mean, specifically, the murder of six million Jews by the Germans. Genocide, a word coined in 1944, signifies the destruction of any ethnic or racial group. Post–World War II genocide has occurred in Cambodia, Rwanda, Iraq, and Bosnia. Sadly, the world has not seen the last one.

This historical event informs almost all of Wiesel's writing. His desire to engrave the memory of the Holocaust deeply into the world's knowledge and conscience in order to prevent future genocide has been Wiesel's life work. Wiesel believes that the Holocaust is so singular an episode in twentieth-century history that only a survivor is capable of creatively writing about it. The great novelists of the twentieth century avoided it out of respect toward the dead and the survivors as well.

Even for those who did not experience it, both gentiles and Jews, the Holocaust has made it much harder to have faith in God or belief in an intrinsic goodness in humanity. Furthermore, the question of responsibility will never be answered satisfactorily because in the broadest sense, hundreds of millions of people worldwide were involved in the crime—from the police who rounded up Jews for shipment to the camps to the world leaders who turned a blind eye to the slaughter—and the indifferent populations who refused to give sanctuary and shelter to the helpless and friendless Jews of Europe.

The Holocaust had many roots: growing anti-Semitism in late nineteenth-century and early twentieth-century Europe, especially in Austria, Poland, the Russian Empire, and its successor, the Soviet Union; but also in the Balkan nations, Germany, and even in France, as evidenced by the Dreyfus Affair (1894–1906), in which a Jewish officer in the French army was wrongly convicted of treason and sent to the penal colony on Devil's Island. The trial, subsequent retrial, and ultimate pardon brought virulent French anti-Semitism to the surface.

Fantastic pseudoscientific racial theories current in the late nineteenth and early twentieth centuries depicted the Jews as an inferior and degenerate race that was polluting "pure" European stocks. France and Great Britain, in their reluctance to stem German rearming in the lull between the two World Wars, and their subsequent appeasement of Hitler in the late 1930s, also were a part of the prelude to the Holocaust.

Most significant, however, was the rise of Adolf Hitler to full dictatorial power over Germany. Early in 1933, Hitler became the German chancellor. He had built the National Socialist Party, the Nazis, on the basis of his rabid hatred of the Jewish people, first fully evidenced in *Mein Kampf* (1923), his master plan to make Germany the dominant country in Europe. Quickly Hitler secured full dictatorial power and opened Germany's first concentration camps, including Dachau, Buchenwald—where Wiesel would later be imprisoned—and Ravensbrück for women. Also in 1933: the Nazis decreed that Jews and descendants of Jews were non-Aryan and could no longer own land; Hitler and the Nazis established the Gestapo, and ordered the burning of hundreds of thousands of books written by Jews, Socialists, and writers the Nazis considered decadent; Hitler announced that the Nazi Party would be the only German political party; the Nazis ordered forced sterilization of people found to have genetic defects.

The next year, Hitler took the title of führer, and ninety percent of the German electorate approved his usurpation of full and unchallenged power. In 1935, Hitler imposed the infamous Nuremberg Race Laws on German Jews. Jews were stripped of educational and business opportunities and civil rights. In 1938, the Austrian people welcomed Hitler and the German army, and Austria entered a union with Germany. Two hundred thousand Austrian Jews fell into Hitler's demonic power. Mauthausen concentration camp was constructed. Jews had to register their wealth. A League of Nations conference called by the United States and attended by representatives of thirty-two countries discussed the Jewish refugee problem, but no nation was willing to take in any Jews. On the night of November 9, Nazi storm troopers rampaged throughout Germany and destroyed scores of synagogues, killed hundreds of Jews, and beat thousands; the date is forever known as *Kristallnacht.* All Jewish businesses were confiscated, and all Jewish children were banned from schools.

Early in 1939, Germany occupied Czechoslovakia, with its population of three hundred fifty thousand Jews. On September 1, Germany invaded Poland, and World War II commenced. Over two million Polish Jews were now in the power of Hitler and his Jew-hating henchmen. As Poland was conquered, its Jews were ordered into ghettos by railroad stations in order to be ready for further transportation. All adult Jews had to wear a yellow Star of David to mark them and separate them from the rest of the population. Adolf Eichmann, a skilled administrator, rose in the Gestapo hierarchy to take control of Jewish affairs and transportation.

In 1940, the Auschwitz concentration camp in Poland opened, and Germany began to deport its Jewish population to Poland. The German army conquered Denmark, Norway, France, Belgium, Holland, and Luxembourg. Hungry, Romania, and Slovakia joined the Axis and six hundred thousand more Jews fell under Hitler's control. Almost all of Western and Central Europe was in German hands. Jewish ghettos in Kraków, Lodz, and Warsaw, Poland, were sealed off, trapping seven hundred thousand Jews. The next year, the Germans occupied Bulgaria, Yugoslavia, and Greece, bringing two hundred thousand more Jews under Hitler's power. The Germans then invaded the Soviet Union, which had a Jewish population of three million. After the Japanese surprise attack on Pearl Harbor, Hitler declared war on the United States, and the German army began murdering all Jews in captured Soviet areas.

In 1942, the Wannsee Conference in a Berlin suburb planned the "Final Solution"—the extermination of European Jewry. The gas chambers at various concentration camps became operative, and the camps turned into extermination camps. Many Warsaw Ghetto Jews were shipped to the Treblinka death camp. Trainloads of money and valuables stolen from Jews were sent back to Germany.

The estimated number of Jews killed by early 1943 was one million. All Gypsies found were sent to extermination camps. The Kraków Ghetto was wiped out. As the Western Allies moved into Italy, the Germans occupied Rome and northern Italy, bringing thirty-five thousand Italian Jews under their control. In Denmark, the Underground transported more than seven thousand Jews to safety in neutral Sweden.

In 1944, while the Allied armies had landed in France and were driving toward Germany, and as the Soviet army reached Poland, Hungary was occupied by the Germans, who, under Adolf Eichmann, rounded up Hungarian Jews and shipped almost four hundred thousand to their death at Auschwitz. The Swedish diplomat Raoul Wallenberg saved some thirty-three thousand Hungarian Jews by issuing diplomatic papers protecting them. Anne Frank and her family were captured in Amsterdam and transported to Auschwitz. Oskar Schindler saved twelve hundred of his Polish Jewish workers. The Warsaw Ghetto rose up in a third and final battle against the Germans. After weeks of resistance, when the last Jews were killed, the Germans demolished the ghetto. Soon the Soviet army began liberating concentration camps, while some Jewish slave laborers at Auschwitz revolted and destroyed a crematory. As the terrible year ended, the retreating Germans destroyed the death camps.

In 1945, Auschwitz, where two million Jews and other Poles were murdered, was liberated by the Soviet army. The Western Allies liberated Buchenwald, Bergen-Belsen, and Dachau. Hitler committed suicide in a Berlin bunker as the Soviet army closed in, and Germany surrendered unconditionally to all the Allies on May 7, 1945.

The Holocaust was over. Approximately six million Jews, of whom at least one million were children, had been murdered by the Germans and their Austrian, Polish, French, Hungarian, Romanian, Slovakian, Lithuanian, Estonian, and Latvian accomplices.

Wiesel writes that he most often is thinking of the victims of the Holocaust. He says: "Why do I write? To wrench those victims from oblivion. To help the dead vanquish death" (Estess 1980, 116). But a problem for Wiesel, as for other artists concerned with depicting this historical event, is that the Holocaust seems unsuitable for art because it is just too horrible; any representation pales before the realities of the event. And the Holocaust cannot even be called a tragedy in the technical Aristotelian sense, in which a tragic hero falls because of his or her own actions and tragic flaw. The Jews were trapped and helpless; they were not flawed tragic figures. Nothing in their individual characters mattered. They might as well have been engulfed in a natural disaster such as a tidal wave for all they could have done about their fate.

THE GREAT JEWISH BOOKS

Elie Wiesel's preuniversity education was mainly, but not entirely, in the great books of Judaism. In his secondary schooling, he studied history, geography, Latin, and physics. But he has continually refreshed himself in the flowing fountain of knowledge and inspiration he found in the great Jewish books. To this day, he studies the Talmud. Holy Writ is a major background to Wiesel's fiction and other writings.

THE HEBREW BIBLE

Of all the achievements of the Jewish people, the greatest is the writing of the Hebrew Bible (*Bible* means "book"). It is a foundation stone of Western civilization as well as of Judaism itself, Christianity, and Islam, and is the basis for the moral and ethical strictures of all three religions. It provides a cosmology, and it defines the relationship between God and human beings. Christianity calls the Hebrew Bible the Old Testament. The Hebrew Bible may have been written as early as King Solomon's time, the tenth century B.C., or it may have been composed through a gathering of texts and oral traditions during the reign of King Josiah of Judah (641–610 B.C.).

The Hebrew Bible is divided into three parts. The first is the Torah, translated as "teaching" or "law." It contains the first five books of the Bible: Genesis, Exodus, Leviticus, Numbers, and Deuteronomy. They are often called The Books of Moses. Orthodox Jews, such as Wiesel and the Hasids, believe that God revealed these books to Moses. They were not "written" by later scribes, and their teaching, meanings, and truths have never altered. Other Jewish denominations, to varying degrees, see the Bible as a historical document that may or may not reveal God's will. But to all practicing Jews, the Torah, also known as the Pentateuch in Greek, is the Bible's most important part. It contains the Creation, the acceptance of God by the Israelites, and, under the leadership of Moses, the great escape from pharaonic Egypt through the Sinai to the Promised Land. Along the way, God gave Moses the Law on Mount Sinai. The Torah contains the basic code of Jewish civil and religious law.

The second part of the Hebrew Bible is the Neviim, translated as "Prophets." The Prophetic books record Jewish history from the conquest of the land of Canaan to the destruction of the First Holy Temple in Jerusalem in 586 B.C. by the Babylonians. Joshua, Samson, Samuel, Saul, David, Solomon, Isaiah, Jeremiah, and Ezekiel come alive in the books of the Prophets.

The third part of the Hebrew Bible is the Ketuvim, the Writings, or *Hagiographa* in Greek. The Ketuvim is the least important part of the

Bible; it contains Psalms, Proverbs, the Book of Job, the Song of Songs, the Book of Ruth, Lamentations on the destruction of the First Temple, Ecclesiastes, the stories of Esther and Daniel, Ezra, and Nehemiah, and the Chronicles, which summarize Jewish history from Adam to the destruction of the kingdom of Judah and the Babylonian captivity.

Roman Catholic, Protestant, and Eastern Orthodox versions of the Hebrew Bible differ in the number and order of the books.

THE TALMUD

Talmud is Hebrew for "Teaching." There are two compilations, the Babylonian and the Jerusalem. They are the records of academic discussion about Jewish law and the administration of the law. The Babylonian Talmud, dating from about 200 A.D., is three times longer than the Jerusalem Talmud, and is considered more authoritative. The Talmud is based on oral interpretations of the Bible as well as the teachings of early rabbis. The Talmud contains two parts: the Mishna, the compilation of the Oral Law and the commentaries and academic discussions of ancient rabbis; and the Gemara, which comments on the Mishna, expounds its texts, and informs Jews on various subjects. The Talmud requires Jews to live by 617 mitzvahs (spoken blessings, good deeds, instructions).

The Bible and the Talmud have regulated and sustained Jewish life for well over two millennia.

THE KABBALAH

Kabbalah is Hebrew for "Tradition." It generally refers to the books of Jewish mysticism that were produced in the Middle Ages between the thirteenth and fifteenth centuries. Originally, the Kabbalah was part of the oral tradition of Jewish study. It is still read, pondered, and studied, particularly by people interested in the spiritual. Wiesel, partly because of his Hasidic background and partly because he is very much a spiritual person, has long been interested in the Kabbalah. Against his father's wishes, he began to study it as a teenager. Some students of the Kabbalah claim secret knowledge of the occult. A Kabbalist legend exists that there is an oral version of the Torah, given by God to Moses and passed on from generation to generation. It allows people to communicate directly with the Deity, bypassing rabbinical documents, including the Talmud. But most scholars who study the medieval texts of the Kabbalah do so only out of fascination and admiration for the imagination and ingenuity of certain Jewish sages before the Enlightenment.

The Zohar, Hebrew for "brightness," is the main text in the Kabbalah. For Kabbalists, it is the most important Holy text after the Torah and Talmud. The Zohar states that there are two worlds mirroring each other: the spiritual world is the true one, and our world is only an illusion. If God wills, souls may travel back and forth between the worlds and in different lives, seeking to find purification and to serve God in the Deity's desire to save the world from destruction, by preparing it for the coming of the Messiah.

WIESEL AND THE WESTERN LITERARY TRADITION

Elie Wiesel's work as a novelist, essayist, historian, and playwright is in the mainstream of Western writing. As a historical novelist, he uses as his backdrop the horrors of the Holocaust and its aftershocks to produce narratives for his readers primarily in the European languages. The difficult task Wiesel set for himself early on is to create a narrative that, by his art, entwines the reader in his life, especially the time in the concentration camps, knowing that only those who were there can feel what he does. (That, of course, is an existential tenet: we can never feel another human's suffering. We are prisoners of our individual sensory experiences: all we know or can know comes to cognition only through our senses: eyes, ears, nose, skin, and mouth. Even the "wisdom" of the ages in books, or from the mouths of elders, must filter through to us via our humble sensory organs.) There is good reason for humans to feel alienated, alone, and despairing. Elie Wiesel's sad and painful novels are a part of the existentialist canon.

The span of Wiesel's fiction encompasses the history of the Jewish people from 1940 to the present day. The great Jewish events are there: the Holocaust, surviving, the founding of the State of Israel, the Israeli War of Independence, the cold war, the Six-Day War, the Yom Kippur War, the freeing of the Jews of the Soviet Union, and the Arab-Palestinian-Israeli conflict.

Wiesel's vision is a tragic one perforce, and tragedy has been part of the Western literary tradition from the fifth century B.C. to the present. Tragedy is a way of understanding and expressing in a literary form what is seen and comprehended: the power of fate, the limitations of human knowledge, and the inevitability of death. The tragic vision is a reaction to despair. Humans experiencing demonic forces, and suffering anxiety and guilt, like Job on the ash heap or King Lear roaring against nature in the storm on the heath, question not only the existence of God, but the existence of humanity in humankind. Tragedy always probes the achievements and the failures of an individual person, a basically good person, but flawed, who somehow unexpectedly is required to act on the public stage that is history. Collectively, Wiesel's novels may constitute the narration of his personal tragedy. Regardless, tragedy is always instructive in that it shows the stage of history to be always filled with horrors and suffering caused by the struggles of men to have power over others. The Spanish philosopher Miguel Unamuno described the tragic sense of life as an experiential sum of insights, feelings, and intuitions that create a worldview that is part conscious and part unconscious. That view is given to a sense of loss, futility, and despair. Suffering is our lot and our destiny.

Wiesel invites his readers to play chorus to his tragedies (or his tragedy), just as the Bible lets us witness such tragedies as King Saul and the destruction of his household in the books of Samuel. If Wiesel had developed out of the stoic faiths of the Orient, he never would have written as he has. Wiesel does not accept; he struggles even in the face of inevitable loss. He struggles to believe in God and to believe in humankind. Indeed, Western tragedy is ultimately not accepting; it roars like a wounded lion. Wiesel's novels of the Holocaust and its aftermath are acts of defiance against his fate and the fate of his fellow Jews.

As a writer of fiction, Wiesel is a modernist. He sees the world as a wilderness. For him, there does not seem to be a clearly defined universal moral order. Modernist Wiesel is an impressionist. Fragmentation and juxtaposition inform his style. Disruption and chaos rule the world. He grapples with the chaos in an attempt to control it. It is always nighttime in Wiesel's fiction. He sees irrationality everywhere. As a modernist writer, Wiesel understands that as the writer creates the world within his or her text, the reader re-creates it imaginatively within her or his mind. So Wiesel is at pains to build place through imagery, both literal and figurative, as he spins his stories.

As discussed fully in chapter 5, Freudian psychology and archetypal myth pervade Wiesel's fiction. He is as interested in the inner person as he is in the social person, and is as much at home in the unconscious mind as he is in the conscious mind. Thus his novels, complex and dense, are equally concerned with psychology and history.

A major technique of Wiesel is to employ the age-old role of the storyteller to inform, teach, and lead the reader to wisdom. The narrator always has authority. The implied reader seems to be a person of intelligence and good will called upon to judge the lives of Wiesel's protagonists and, with respect to the tragic mode, feel pity for the suffering of individual people and the fate of humankind. He or she must believe in the event and be open to "experiencing" the Holocaust and its aftermath through fiction. Wiesel created a large, worldwide audience of them. That creation, a result of his large body of Holocaust literature, is one of Wiesel's most significant achievements.

Wiesel, the philosophical novelist, legitimizes questioning. It is permissible to demand of God an explanation for the Deity's inability or unwillingness to prevent evil. If God both creates and destroys, may we not do the same? Are destruction and creation inextricably linked? What excuse does God have for the Holocaust? How could God have allowed the destruction of the very people he created to bring redemption and salvation to humankind? That he brought, and continues to bring, an audience to ponder these questions and to attempt answers for themselves may be Wiesel's greatest achievement as a writer.

Part II

The Holocaust
Narratives

3

Night
(1958)

In *Night,* Elie Wiesel writes in the tradition of Franz Kafka, the early twentieth-century Jewish novelist who created a bone-chilling, impressionistic world of guilt, anxiety, and existential isolation (Abrahamson 1985, I:45). The "Night" is the darkness of the Auschwitz concentration camp, the darkness that descended over Europe when the Germans under Hitler began their World War II attempt at world conquest and racial purification, and the blackness of death that engulfed the six million Jews who were the victims of Hitler's monstrous, evil hatred. But night is always followed by the dawn, where light may lead to comprehension, justice, renewal, and, perhaps, forgiveness. The dawn leaves the nightmare behind and allows a new journey to begin.

Like *The Diary of Anne Frank, Night* is a depiction of an aspect of the Holocaust as seen and experienced by a youth, but, unlike Frank's *Diary,* it is written by a mature person, and thus it is infinitely darker and more profound. *Night* may be considered an autobiographical novel or a slightly fictionalized memoir (Wiesel's actual memoirs are discussed later under Autobiography). Some events in the book differ from actual happenings.

Night is so filled with the atmosphere of evil, a description of a Dantean Hell, that it "almost cries out not to be touched, interpreted, synthesized" (Brown 1983, 50). But a major literary work needs to be embraced, searched for significance, and converted to the reader's use as we seek to understand the possible depths of human depravity, the limits of human endurance, and the parameters of the human condition. In *Night,* Wiesel demands that we try to experience what the boy protagonist, Eliezer, feels when he says: "Never shall I forget that night, the first night in the camp, which has turned my life into one long night. . . . Never shall I forget that smoke. Never shall I forget the little faces of the children, whose bodies I saw turned into wreathes of smoke. . . . Never shall I forget those flames which consumed my faith forever" (44).

The reviews of *Night* when it was first published in English were almost all laudatory. However, some critics felt that *Night* was not being judged by the same standards as a work by a writer such as Ernest Hemingway. A. Alvarez, in *Commentary,* called *Night* a defective book. He felt it relied too heavily on overstatement. But he also said: "As a human document *Night* is . . . certainly beyond criticism" (Alvarez 1964, 65). Wesley H. Hager, in *The Christian Century,* called *Night* a work "beyond tears and anger. . . . The record of the shadow that fell upon our boasted civilization in our own time" (Hager 1961, 84).

PLOT DEVELOPMENT

Night tells the story of what happens to a religious Romanian Jewish boy, Eliezer, from late in 1941 through April 1945. The story is one of maturation and of a double journey, spiritual and geographical. Eliezer has had a happy childhood in the little town of Sighet, surrounded by a loving family—mother, father, three sisters—and immersed in a supportive religious community. He devotes himself to the study of the Talmud and then to the Kabbalah, despite his father's opinion that the study of mystical books is not right for a young Jewish man.

Eliezer's life is truly sheltered. But the world is closing in on Sighet, and the Jews are in psychological flight from truth and the terrible reality that has engulfed their coreligionists almost everywhere else in Europe. Eliezer's elderly Hasidic mentor and friend, Moché the Beadle, has escaped the German killers in Poland after witnessing the execution of Jewish men, women, and children, and has tried to warn the people of Sighet that their lives are in grave danger, but the townspeople, to Moché's horror, believe he is mad and refuse to act on his alarm. On the other hand, what could they do? Where could they go in German-occupied Europe? Death was waiting everywhere. If Eliezer's father had listened to his son (who believed Moché's report and suggested they flee), sold his business, and led his family to Palestine when the way was still open, they just might have escaped the Holocaust. But the father believed he was too old to pull up roots and start over again.

When the Nazi ring of death closes in on his world in the fall of 1944, Eliezer, his family, and all the Jews of Sighet are herded into a small ghetto area. Soon the boy finds himself jammed into a railway car filled with his family and neighbors, on the way to the Birkenau reception camp and the neighboring Auschwitz concentration camp in Poland. In the railway car, eighty people, given little food and water and hardly able to breathe, struggle to stay alive. One elderly woman becomes hysterical as she envisions flames and furnaces, a portent of what awaits the deportees.

Arriving at the concentration camp, Eliezer and his father are separated from his mother and sisters. He will never see his mother and one of his sisters again. The man and the boy, healthy and strong, are selected for slave labor and marched to Buna, another camp. Their last view of Auschwitz is of infants being thrown into a burning pit to be roasted to death. Eliezer, despairing, considers suicide by running onto an electric fence, but does not do it.

Eliezer, his father, and all the worker prisoners are beaten and starved. Their heads have been shaved. Numbers have been tattooed on their arms. They are no longer human beings; they are merely slave numbers. The men are marched to a factory at nearby Buna where they labor in a warehouse sorting electrical parts. The guards, some of them prisoners themselves, are sadistic. A doctor demands Eliezer's gold crown, but the boy manages to save it for a while; soon, however, a foreman extorts it from him by threatening Eliezer's father if the son does not relinquish the tiny piece of gold.

A prisoner-guard takes a dislike to Eliezer, beats him, and has him whipped. Eliezer sees a thirteen-year-old boy hanged; the boy is so light that it takes thirty minutes for him to strangle. When a prisoner asks where God is, Eliezer replies: "He is hanging here on this gallows" (62). Slowly human dignity withers away, and the imprisoned men descend to savagery or depressed numbness in the face of daily horrors. Still, Eliezer matures, shows compassion, and, along with his father, maintains some shred of humanity. Despite degradation and humiliation, the boy never sinks to the predatory and savage level that some half-demented guards and prisoners descend to. Eliezer may be in hell, but he neither swears allegiance nor takes out citizenship. When Germans throw bread at the prisoners to see them fight for it, and sons beat fathers for a piece of the bread, Eliezer and his father remain mutually caring. Father and son support each other as best they can.

When the Soviet army approaches Buna, the slave laborers must make a forty-two-mile forced march to the Gleiwitz camp in the bitter winter of January 1945. Those who are too weak to keep up are shot by the Germans. During the march, Eliezer injures his foot. His father bandages the foot and saves his son from freezing to death. Strength and resolve to survive begin to wither. As the Soviet army comes even closer, the slave workers endure a ten-day train journey in an open cattle car to Germany's Buchenwald concentration camp. The noble, nurturing father, despite Eliezer's attempt to save him, finally succumbs to dysentery and a savage beating. The boy has been separated from his dying father, so he is not sure that his father was really dead when the body was taken to be burned in the ovens. Alone, Eliezer desperately struggles to survive. He can do so because he has been relieved of the burden of caring for his father. Guiltily, he remembers that the last word his father said to him was "Eliezer" (106).

The boy's physical journey has nearly destroyed his body, and his spiritual journey has led him only to despair and an abandonment of the God he had loved so much. Eliezer is in deep depression, expecting at any moment to be killed. When Buchenwald is liberated on April 10, 1945, by American troops, all Eliezer can think of is getting something to eat. Ironically, he contracts food poisoning. A few days later, when he recovers, a look into a mirror confirms that he is virtually a corpse. That is what the months of suffering and starvation have done to the sixteen-year-old boy.

SETTING

In *Night,* Wiesel employs a first-person narrative as Eliezer tells the story of his early life in Sighet and his concentration camp experiences. The prose is sparse, direct, unornamented—like evidence in a trial, or like a thoughtful documentary. Itzhak Ivry, in *Saturday Review,* states that "there is a unique quality in the experiences of a child in hell. Mr. Wiesel writes in short, staccato sentences, in the simplest words, and in a relentless, self-denying effort to tell the whole truth" (Ivry 1960, 23).

Characterization is select, minimalist, but vivid. The places in the novel are clearly depicted. *Night* has two worlds, and morally they are worlds apart. The Transylvanian world of the town of Sighet seems almost Garden of Eden-like in its innocence compared to the hell that is the world of the concentration camps. The contrast between these two worlds makes for much of the power of the novel. No Holocaust writer has achieved the level of verisimilitude in depicting the horror of the camps that Wiesel did in his first narrative. The concentration camps transcend reality. They constitute a metaphysical terrain, a nether region, a Dantean Inferno, where a boy sees into a Conradian "Heart of Darkness." In other words, Wiesel's sulfurous descriptions are fired in his imagination and they smash their way into ours.

The authenticity of the depictions of a Romanian village as the noose tightened around the trapped Jewish community, and of the horrifying camps, leaves lasting memories in the readers. Night, dark and seemingly unending; night, the opposite of light that is the source of hope; night is the great overriding, all-encompassing symbol of Wiesel's first narrative.

CHARACTER DEVELOPMENT

Two characters dominate the novel; almost all other characters are two-dimensional. Eliezer, the protagonist of the novel, undergoes the most profound of changes from a religious, spiritual, God-loving boy to an ageless person, wise and sad far beyond his years, broken in body and spirit, and one who has seen the very architectonics of his life completely undermined. He is washed up on the shore of the future, but all of his past—except memory—is swept away in the deadly deluge.

The name *Eliezer* means "God has granted my prayer." It seems an ironic name considering Eliezer's experiences in the Holocaust, but it calls for reflection: Is the prayer a prayer for survival? Eliezer does survive. Or is it a prayer to be able to understand the human condition, to accept what has happened, to be given the chance to remember the dead? Eliezer is given that opportunity. But most of all, Eliezer learns the depths of depravity inherent in the human animal. And he learns to hate. Initially, Eliezer cannot believe his eyes. "So fundamental is the horror to which he is an eyewitness that seeing comes at the expense of his bodily awareness of himself as a vital and perceiving entity" (Hamaoui 1990, 122). Eliezer's very adolescence permits him to grasp the scope of the cruelty he encounters, because he is so thoroughly unprepared for it.

In the camps, Eliezer must struggle to keep as healthy as possible because he wants to live. And he must help to keep his father alive because as long as father and son are together, they are a family, and their strength is greater than two. Eliezer remains compassionate; he does kind deeds when he can. Near the end of the narrative, however, Eliezer, believing himself and the Jewish people abandoned by God, hopeless and broken by the death of his father, nearly dead from starvation, awaits his own death in a state of torpor. When the Americans liberate the camp, he eats until he is sick, and recovering, is able to look at himself in a mirror for the first time since his incarceration. He sees what the world has done to him.

Eliezer's father, Chlomo, is a business person and a leader of the Jewish community. He is an Orthodox Jew but not a Hasid. He tries to help his fellow Jews and is even imprisoned for a while for aiding Jewish refugees. His failing is that he refuses to believe the information and the evidence that the Germans are planning a genocide for the Jews of his country. The idea that Hitler planned to exterminate the entire Jewish community of Europe was inconceivable to him and to most Eastern European Jews. Hitler seemed just another oppressor in the long, sad history of Jews as victims of anti-Semitism. The logistics of murdering millions of people seemed beyond credibility. The Jews of Europe, and the world, underestimated German technology and efficiency.

Eliezer's father, Chlomo, is an Abraham, a Jewish patriarch, who leads Eliezer, a faithful and believing Isaac, to the sacrifice of the scapegoat (the Jew); but instead of father and son surviving because of God's mercy, the father loses his life and the son loses his faith. The father is also a Moses figure, who, without God's guidance but under orders of the satanic Hitler, leads the Jewish people of Sighet on an exodus. However, it is not to the Promised Land they hope for—resettlement in the "East"—but to the gas chamber and the flames of the crematory.

In the dark hours of their last days together, the father supports and sustains his son—his biological future—for as long as he is able. Then the child becomes the father to the man in his last hours. Together, father and son personify the bond that can tie a loving, caring, and respectful relationship into a bundle of strength that has at least the possibility of riding out the fiercest storm imaginable. Eliezer's father is a quiet hero. He has made mistakes, however: Forewarned of the murderous German intentions, he does not try to rescue his family and himself. Some of his coreligionists would fault him for not being religious enough, but no quantity of religious fervor saved any Jew in the hands of the Germans, and very few Jews managed to escape. Secularists and Hasidim, side by side, no longer in theological dispute, stumbled together to their deaths.

Chlomo's heroism consisted of sheltering his young son, fighting the boy's despair, and giving the child something immediate to live for, the survival of the one member of his family he was sure was alive. In Hasidic terms, to save one life is to save all humanity. When his son's survival is at risk because of his own failing health, the father, having done all that love can do, and duty served, disappears into the night.

One minor character is of significance: Moché the Beadle, who undergoes a profound change in the story. Moché takes care of the Hasidic synagogue in Sighet. An awkward, clownish man, he walks barefoot, sings aloud much of the time, and studies the Kabbalistic books. Moché becomes Eliezer's instructor in these books of Jewish mysticism. In 1942, Moché is in the first group of Jews deported by the Hungarian police to be turned over to the Germans for extermination. He miraculously escapes execution in Poland and returns to Sighet to warn the Jews of the town that they will be murdered after they are deported. The townspeople think him mad, or looking for pity. The once happy, religious enthusiast is now a prophet of doom, and the townspeople choose not to believe his prophecy, because they dare not believe it. It is too horrible to contemplate and, basically, they are trapped. They can escape only in their hope and in their dreams.

Weary of speaking of the danger, and like the Trojan Cassandra who was fated to reveal the future and not be heeded, Moché fades from the narrative. His last words to the Jews of Sighet, as they are being rounded up for the new deportations are: "I warned you" (20). Then he flees.

THEMATIC ISSUES

The most important theme in *Night* is that of theodicy: the struggle to believe in God's justice and goodness when the world created by the Deity is so filled with evil. The boy, Eliezer, lived in a Jewish world where God was loved and the people were peaceful and good. Ironically and tragically, the faith of the Jews of Sighet debilitated them and led them into the hands of their destroyers (Berenbaum 1979, 12). Taken from that sheltering world, the boy is thrust into the night of Nazi power and values. He has no way to handle the presence of evil. Prayers are of no avail. He does not even have the comfort and guidance of his holy books. Trying to praise God while witnessing the horror and torture in the camps is like filling his mouth with ashes. Jewish values are destroyed in the concentration camps, and the Messiah does not come to save anyone. The prisoners cry out in bitterness: "Where is God now?"(76) So Eliezer revolts against God. He must reestablish his faith in another time and place. In a sense, all the rest of Wiesel's fiction tells the story of Eliezer's (Wiesel's) struggle with God and his return to belief in the existence of the Deity, even if he can never quite forgive God.

A second major theme in *Night* is man's inhumanity to man. The sixteen-year-old boy witnesses how cruel human beings can be to other human beings; how easy it is to dehumanize our fellow humans; how even the tortured can torture others; how, in the face of fear and hunger, fathers and sons may savage each other. The vividly depicted apocalyptic abominations of the Germans, a supposedly civilized people, cause Eliezer and Wiesel to lose faith not only in God's goodness, but also in humankind's capacity for goodness. The most painful message the reader must absorb from the text is that degradation, humiliation, torture, starvation, and unrelenting suffering do not bring out the best in people. Most often, they reduce human beings to animal-like savagery as they struggle to save themselves. We are not saints.

Another major theme in *Night* is the father-son relationship. In the concentration camp, Chlomo and Eliezer represent the family stripped down to two. Their love anchors them. Mutual support sustains them for a while in the face of unimaginable evil; it is the keel of their humanness binding them together, and it maintains the life force that prevents suicide. When the prisoners must undertake the forced march in the snow from Buna to Gleiwitz, and Eliezer is in so much pain from his injured foot that death seems a desired relief, it is the presence of his father, and his father's need for him, that keeps Eliezer in the struggle for life. Human beings will do much for love. Eliezer knows he "has no right to die" (92). When the boy collapses, his father protects him. Later, when someone is strangling Eliezer, his father calls upon a strong friend and they save the boy. Then Eliezer saves his living father from being placed among the dead to be burned. Who would do more for us than our own flesh and blood?

There is a beauty in *Night,* despite the grimness. It resides in the determination of a boy not to break his covenant with his father even if God has broken the covenant with the Jewish people (Estess 1980, 25). Finally, tragically, Eliezer cannot save his dying father. When the boy returns from work one day, his father is gone, taken to the crematory, perhaps still alive. Eliezer, who sometimes, naturally, wished to be relieved of the burden of his dying father, is left with a lifetime of guilt because he could not save his father—who had given him life and who had saved his life again and again—from what all fathers must endure: death. Other fathers and sons in the camps do not behave as lovingly as Eliezer and his father, for the Germans purposely dehumanized their prisoners, encouraged bestial behavior, so they could think of the wretched people as mere animals.

A minor theme in *Night* is the question of the role of the State of Israel in the matter of Jewish survival. Of course, Wiesel wrote *Night* after the establishment of the Jewish state. In *Night,* Eliezer wants his father to take the family to Palestine before they have to face the German, Hungarian, and Romanian fascists. In the concentration camps, Eliezer and other young Jewish prisoners discuss moving to Palestine after liberation. Wiesel, perhaps unconsciously, is introducing in *Night* a pervasive theme in his fiction: Israel as the much-needed protector of the Jewish people, the strong guarantor of Jewish survival in a continually hostile world.

ALTERNATE READING: A READER-RESPONSE READING

Reader-Response criticism came into focus in the 1970s. It is concerned with, and it attempts to describe, what happens in the mind of the reader when he or she is reading fiction. Reader-response criticism insists that each reading is different from any other, and thus a literary text makes possible an infinite number of versions and meanings. The mind creates the text, and the mind is also the primary critical instrument. As it creates, it interprets.

For a reader-response critic, there is no single meaning in a literary text. There is a certain relativity in reading. Readings are not "correct" or "incorrect." Language is the medium of meaning, and it is subjective. It does not replicate reality; it recalls, shapes, comments on, and even foretells reality. The literary text first exists and is edited in the writer's mind. The transference through written language to the reader's mind must alter the text because the life experiences and cultural backgrounds of the writer and the readers differ. In a way, the text has gaps that the reader fills in with his or her experience, making the story his or her story—and now a part of the reader's experience. This process is a significant part of the aesthetic pleasure of reading fiction.

Thus the work of the reader-response critic is to find out how the text is "read." Some reader-response critics point out the ways different readers read the texts differently. Other reader-response critics— reception theorists—believe that the significance of a text lies in what the author is trying to get the reader to feel or to do and how the reader reacts to that effort. Cultural materialists argue that the reading depends on the context in which it occurs; a seemingly stable literary text could be, indeed is, read quite differently in different cultures and epochs. Texts and their readings may be sites of cultural contestation.

In *Night*, Wiesel attempts, with considerable success, to evoke an empathetic response in the reader to the concentration camp experience. Without malice, Wiesel wishes the memory of the Holocaust to haunt us. He expects the reader to become, through the process of reading, both victim and persecutor in order for him or her to realize that both roles are possible in all human beings. After *Night*, Eliezer's Auschwitz endures in our mind. In the process of writing *Night*, an action that followed a long gestation period, Wiesel, unconsciously perhaps, invented himself: Elie Wiesel the spokesperson and chief mourner for the nameless murdered Jews of the Holocaust, and Elie Wiesel the conscience of the Western world.

4

Dawn
(1961)

Dawn, Elie Wiesel's second novel, extends the narration of survival, but it is not autobiographical. Still, Wiesel continues the battle between the desire to find peace in death and the desire to survive and continue life (Berenbaum 1979, 26). It is always more difficult to live than to die when one is suffering and the world seems hopelessly antagonistic. Despite its title, *Dawn* is a dark novel. Early dawn, at least, is more darkness than light. As in *Night,* once more the innocent suffer without reason, and God does not interfere.

Dawn is a short novel about how a victim may be required to become a victimizer and how difficult that transition can be (Fine 1982, 35). *Dawn* is also a novel about the ambiguities of the question of right and wrong, the loss of innocence, and the realization that killing marks a person for life. Elisha, the protagonist, has choices—free will—and he chooses to follow duty over conscience. Even though the cause he serves is just, his execution of a British army officer in retribution for the hanging of a Jewish prisoner of war is a terrible act, so absolutely terrible that it also indicts the phantoms of his life, a congregation of the dead: "those who had formed him. In murdering a man I was making them murderers" (55). In other words, if one kills a human being, then one's ancestors are accessories to the crime. The angry Elisha wants God judged, not himself, but his silence instead of refusal and his act indict him, not God. Wiesel the existentialist always insists that one is responsible for one's actions. Furthermore, Wiesel implies that through the cold-blooded killing of a person the killer knows well and does not hate, the killer, as a manifestation of guilt and repentance, comes to identify with the slain person. In the end, as requested by the British soldier, Elisha will mail the man's last letter to his son in England. It is an act of kindness and a manifestation of guilt.

Dawn is unashamedly ambivalent as Wiesel debates the right and wrong of killing in a good cause. Herbert Mitgang, in the *New York Times Book Review,* states that "*Dawn* is a book that hits home at the unsentimental heart, a strong morality tale written from the inside" (Mitgang 1961, 23).

PLOT DEVELOPMENT

In *Dawn,* Wiesel introduces a new protagonist, Elisha, whose background is similar to Eliezer's in *Night* and to Wiesel's. Elisha is a Jewish young man between his eighteenth and nineteenth birthdays living in post–World War II Palestine under British Mandate control. Elisha has barely survived the Buchenwald concentration camp. He is a Lazarus brought back to life. However, he does not think of himself as a survivor, but as one of the dead even though he breathes. He says paradoxically, "I had died and come back to earth, dead" (51).

While studying philosophy at the Sorbonne in Paris, unable and unwilling to return home to his village in Eastern Europe because it is now occupied by hostile Russians, Elisha is visited by a man named Gad who, mysteriously, asks the boy to devote his life to him. Gad is a sabra, that is, a Jew born in what was then called Palestine. Gad sounds like God in name and like God's messenger in his words. He recruits Elisha for an unnamed Jewish terrorist organization of one hundred Jews, mostly Holocaust survivors, who are determined to drive the British out of Palestine and create a Jewish state. Elisha joins up because he has lost everyone, is deeply depressed, and, not caring if he lives or dies, seemingly has nothing to lose. He feels that perhaps in the terrorist gang, he will find family even if he cannot find God.

Elisha becomes a boy soldier in the extremist group, working in the Jewish underground. He makes friends with a few comrades, including Gad, who was his recruiter, and Gad's girlfriend, Ilana, the clandestine radio voice of the Jewish rebellion. Elisha kills British soldiers in action; that is a soldier's work, and the soldier risks his own life while doing his duty. Then, because the British intend to hang a wounded Jewish prisoner, the leader of the guerrilla force calls for a British soldier to be kidnapped and held hostage in an attempt to prevent the hanging of the Jewish prisoner of war.

A British army captain, foolishly strolling out alone one night, is kidnapped and held prisoner; Captain John Dawson is a career soldier, about forty years old, married, with a son at Cambridge University. The terrorists announce their plan to execute Dawson if the Jewish soldier is hanged, hoping to prevent the judicial murder of a Jewish prisoner. The British refuse to commute the sentence of the Jew, and as he is hanged. Elisha, who has briefly come to know Dawson during the long night they have spent together, is told to shoot him. He obeys the order. Then Elisha must live with the guilt of having killed a decent man in cold blood only because he was a political enemy. Independence, freedom, and survival require a terrible price from those young people who are ordered to kill for them. When the killing is a cold-blooded assassination, devoid of the hot, raging blood-lust of fearful battle, a young fighter faces a lifetime of bad dreams, doubts, regrets, and self-recrimination.

SETTING

In *Dawn*, Wiesel employs a first-person narrative as Elisha tells the story of his post–concentration camp experiences in the British Mandate of Palestine as native Palestinian Jews and Holocaust survivors fight the English for control of the land, some of which will become the State of Israel. The prose is sparse, direct, and with limited ornamentation; it is much like an interior dialogue. Iterative eye imagery structures the narrative. Elisha thinks of death as a creature with great eyes searching out its victims. He is afraid of looking into the eyes of the man he must execute. He also fears that one day a son of his will look into his eyes and see the face of John Dawson (60). Elisha believes that a hangman wears a mask so that those about to be hanged see only the eyes of coming death. He who has seen so much death and hated it has become the angel of death himself.

Dawn is a very tight, confined narrative. Characterization is minimalist but vivid. A very large part of the novel is set in the terrorists' hideout. The story could easily be adapted for the stage: There are few developed characters. Family ghosts could be off-stage voices. The narrator coldly relates all the expository, preceding events. The places of the novel, outside of the hideout, are not clearly depicted. Jerusalem and other parts of Palestine seem unreal, because the novel is to a large extent an allegory for the post-Holocaust Jewish struggle between the inherent pacifism of a people who have been commanded "Thou shalt not kill" and the need to fight and even kill in order to survive as individuals and as a nation.

CHARACTER DEVELOPMENT

The name *Elisha* comes from the Hebrew Bible. Elisha is the prophet who succeeds the prophet Elijah. Perhaps the character Elisha in *Dawn* succeeds the character Eliezer in *Night,* and is the prophet of the new Jewishness with its determinism to establish and maintain a Jewish state against all odds and all enemies. But Elisha is still a part of old European Jewry. His childhood was a religious one. Once he had lived for God, but God did not live for him. He tries to think of himself as a freedom fighter, but eventually he comes to realize that he is merely a murderer. He is an existential killer without passion. A gun in hand compels one, despite reason, to use it. The shot that kills the English officer damns Elisha: "The earth yawned beneath my feet and I seemed to be falling into a bottomless pit" (16). And it kills him too: "There was a pain in my head and my body was growing heavy.... It's done. I've killed. I've killed Elisha" (90). The final image in the novel is that of Elisha seeing his reflection in a mirror and being horrified by the sight. He sees an image of death the slayer: "The face was my own" (90). Elisha now has, and will continue to have, the eyes of death.

Gad is an enigmatic figure. Elisha sees him as fate come knocking, a messenger from God sent to give purpose to Elisha's life and to change pacifistic Jews into Joshua-like conquerors of the new Canaan, the Palestine of modern times. Gad's message is that Jews can afford no longer to be better, more moral, than other people, for if they should continue that way, they will come to an end. They must fight fiercely for their homeland and be willing to shed the blood of their enemies while risking their own lives. Gad will lead Elisha to the red dawn in Palestine.

Captain John Dawson, the British Army officer kidnapped by the Jewish terrorists and held hostage against the life of the condemned Jewish prisoner, seems a somewhat improbable characterization. As previously noted, he is taken captive when out strolling by himself one evening, a rather careless act during a guerilla war. He is described as a handsome, distinguished man in his early forties. He is not afraid. He is actually sorry for Elisha, his executioner. Elisha cannot bring himself to hate the man, even though he is Elisha's enemy. He does hate that Dawson is going to make him a murderer. Dawson really does not know why he is to die, and Elisha is not sure either. Dawson dies trying to tell Elisha a funny story and saying the name "Elisha." In *Night,* the father's last word is "Eliezer." Wiesel perhaps is implying that Elisha's killing of an older man, a father with a son his age, is a symbolic parricide. Regardless, Elisha has murdered, and murder is not one of the duties of a soldier—killing in battle, yes; but not murder.

Furthermore, Dawson deserved some recognition for being a member of an army that fought Hitler at a time when no one else dared. The British army in World War II captured concentration camps and saved some of the remnants of European Jewry. Surely, the British behavior toward Jewish survivors after the war was reprehensible, but it could not erase the fact that Britain made very great sacrifices to help save Western civilization from a long night of fascist tyranny.

Ilana, the radio Voice of Freedom and Gad's girlfriend, is a compassionate young woman who understands Elisha's fear of the approaching night when he will have to kill John Dawson, and who attempts to assuage Elisha's suffering. She comforts him with her softness and her caring. She tells him that he will get over the trauma of what he has been ordered to do, and that one day the English will leave Palestine and the Jews will have their own country again. She assures him that their war is a holy war. Ilana's voice is like a mother's. It is also "like the voice of God" with the power to "impart a vision of the future" (63). But Elisha cannot accept her comfort, because he knows in his soul that he will never forget the cold-blooded shooting of an unarmed human being whom he does not hate, and he will never forgive himself. Blood is on his hands. Nations are born in blood, and freedom is won with blood. But the victors still pay their price.

THEMATIC ISSUES

A major theme in *Dawn* is the need of the Jewish people to abandon nineteen centuries of pacifism in order to fight their enemies instead of running away or meekly succumbing to them. It is painful for Wiesel to embrace this doctrine, but he has seen the ultimate cost of pacifism. Being a people without a country has cost world Jewry dearly: centuries of persecution, and in the twentieth century, the plundering and murder of six million people in only twelve years. In *Dawn,* Jews must not only fight those who would deprive them of their biblical inheritance, the return to their ancestral home, but also pay the penalty of blood: remorse and guilt over killing, cold-blooded or not.

Three thousand five hundred years ago, God said, "Thou shalt not kill." Only Jews listened to God, and it cost them dearly. Now they too must abandon the commandment or be driven to extinction by those who hate them enough to murder them only for being who they are. The novel's title, *Dawn,* symbolizes an awakening, the dawn of a new Jewish person, steeled by the violence of World War II, willing to fight and die for the Holy Land. The dawn of the state, Israel, will come about through the efforts and sacrifices of those young people like Elisha who renounced their religious training and took up arms for the new-old nation that, after the partition of Palestine, was recognized by the United Nations in 1948.

A second significant theme in *Dawn* is the questioning of the relevance and the justification of political assassination, especially for the purposes of terrorizing and taking revenge. Although hardly more than a boy, Elisha must kill Dawson. In doing so, he loses his innocence and becomes an unwilling angel of death. He will live with his guilt forever. The very telling of the tale, in the first person, from a point in Elisha's future, indicates the confessional nature of the novel. Wiesel is somewhat ambivalent on the theme, but his judgment, one may finally infer, comes down against the act.

ALTERNATE READING: A NEW HISTORICIST READING

In the 1980s, New Historicism, in the name of cultural criticism, revived the early twentieth-century investigation of historical background as a tool of literary criticism, methodology that was discredited and supplanted by Formalist New Criticism in the 1940s (see chapter 7, Alternate Reading: A Formalist Reading). The latter insisted that objective, internal textual analysis was the only worthwhile critical concern.

"Old" historicism focused on the historical, political, religious, and cultural background of a literary text at the expense of close reading for interpretation and aesthetic analysis. New historicism, influenced by Marxist critical theory (see chapter 10: Alternate Reading: A Marxist Critical Reading), like its venerable ancestor, is less interested in the actual literary text than in the text's use as one of many cultural representations of a time and place that influenced, and was influenced by, the political, social, and economic forces in society. New Historicism searches for the connections between text and time. Moreover, cultural representations tend to reinforce dominant power, initially in the societies in which they are first read, and later, in the societies in which they have become "classics."

The novel *Dawn* depicts a fictional—but clearly representational—moment in the violent birth of the State of Israel as Jewish extremists resort to retaliatory violence in their ultimately successful attempt to drive the British army out of Palestine, so that the Jewish state could come into being. Wiesel, basically a pacifistic thinker, has mixed feelings about this method of achieving statehood, despite his sympathy for the surviving remnants of European Jewry trying to create a safe haven for themselves in the homeland promised to the Jews by God and the British Balfour Declaration of 1917.

Wiesel's only offhanded mentioning of the Arab population of Mandate Palestine is unfair to a people who also have rights in the land despite their support of Nazi Germany in World War II and their history of persecuting Jews. Elisha's actions seem antithetical to the moral precepts of Judaism. The reader cannot approve of Elisha's actions, and Wiesel is at least ambivalent about those actions.

Dawn may also be faulted in that the portrayal of Captain Dawson, a British army career officer on duty in Palestine, in 1946 or 1947 would have served in one of the Allied armies that liberated the concentration camps and saved the lives of many Jews. Then, to placate the rebellious Arab population of Palestine, a population supporting its own terrorists, the British authorities attempted to keep Holocaust survivors out of the Holy Land. Still, the British valiantly fought the Germans, at first almost alone, from 1939 to 1945. It was General Bernard Montgomery and the British Eighth Army at the 1942 Battle of El Alamein in Egypt who prevented the Germans from conquering Palestine and destroying the Jewish community there too. This historical fact deserved some mention in the text. So *Dawn* inadvertently contains subversive energies as it both serves the ideological needs of post–World War II Jewry and deconstructs the received perception of a persecuted people solely without blame in the still boiling cauldron of Middle East politics.

5

The Accident
(1962)

Because the unnamed narrator in *The Accident* has the same background as Eliezer in *Night,* perhaps the original title of the novel, *Le Jour (The Day),* was a better one because it more clearly links *The Accident* with *Night.* Furthermore, Elisha in *Dawn* has much the same Holocaust background. Loosely speaking, the three protagonists almost seem to be the same person as the extended narrative advances in time and moves from night to dawn to day.

The Accident is the story of a Jewish man's painful, sometimes delirious, recovery from being struck and nearly killed by a taxi at Times Square in New York City as he was crossing the street with his former lover and now depressed friend, Kathleen. The Holocaust survivor, a reporter at the United Nations who is about thirty years old, must fight to survive again, and he does not seem to want to. He is angry and filled with guilt because he survived the Holocaust and his family did not (Fine 1982, 33).

The Accident is also a story of love found, lost, and found again: a love made possible by a woman's devotion to a man who is not sure he wants to go on with his life and who is convinced that he never will be happy again. As always, Wiesel's story shows little cynicism about God or human beings even when he is describing the Holocaust or showing life afterward for survivors (Leddy 1990, 47).

The two major questions of the novel are: Can the survivor of the pain and suffering of the Holocaust, and the pain and suffering of a terrible accident, still affirm life? and Will the dead ever leave us to our own lives and be forgotten so we can go on living without guilt? The narrator's lifelong struggle, after the loss of his family and his home, is locating his own identity: "You want to know who I am, truly? I don't know myself" (73). And we never learn his name. *The Accident* marks the true beginning of Wiesel's depiction of the struggle back to life of the prototypical Holocaust survivor, a process that, at this writing, is still going on for many elderly people.

Reviews of *The Accident* varied in judgments. John C. Pine, in *Library Journal,* complimented Wiesel's use of flashbacks as being particularly skillful (Pine 1962, 996). Herbert Mitgang, in the *New York Times Book Review,* was impressed by Wiesel's willingness to "tackle the largest themes" including "Nazi brutality and the vestiges of war," but he also saw the novel as "falsely melodramatic" (Mitgang 1963, 26).

PLOT DEVELOPMENT

The plot of *The Accident* is convoluted. The novel begins with the announcement that an accident has taken place. The narrator describes the minutes before the accident happens: his walk to Times Square with Kathleen, who, we later find out, had been his lover and who, after a brief, loveless marriage to another man, is trying to reestablish a relationship with the narrator, whom she has continued to love. They argue about which movie to see. Kathleen is pushing too hard to rekindle their affair. The narrator would like to run away, not only from Kathleen and the problems of contemporary life, but from the haunting memories of the dead that sear his heart.

The couple start to cross a busy street on a green light, Kathleen walking a little ahead, always trying to lead him. But to where? The movie she wants to see and the relationship she wants the reluctant narrator to accept. The narrator hears a woman's scream, and the next thing he remembers is that he is lying on his back in the street. His mouth is full of blood, many bones are broken, he is bleeding internally, he has a brain concussion, and he is very near death. Much later, when he is no longer in critical condition, he learns from Kathleen that a speeding taxi had hit him and dragged him several yards. In the hospital, he undergoes five hours of emergency surgery and he remains unconscious for five days. The description of the narrator's hospital ordeal, based on Wiesel's experience in 1956, is vivid. The narrator must fight death for the life in his body as he struggled against the Germans in the camps, but he is a poor resister now, because he has little will to live.

While in great pain, he remembers the night he met Kathleen. It was at the ballet in Paris where a friend introduced him to a beautiful girl speaking French with an American accent. A spark flew between them and they felt as if they had known each other for a long time. Their first conversation as they walk by the River Seine at night is about the narrator's beloved grandmother, who was gassed and her body burned at Auschwitz. It is a prophetic conversation because the ghost of the grandmother haunts the narrator and endangers the relationship from the beginning. In a mystical way, the grandmother's soul is loose in the world because she was never buried. The ashes of her burned body still float in the atmosphere. Until the narrator can make peace with the memory of his murdered grandmother, the lovers' bed is as cold as a grave.

After this recollection, the narrative returns to the days in the hospital. The narrator is racked with thirst, but is not allowed to drink despite high fever: the water would cause him to vomit, thus interfering with the massive medications he is on. In the fever, the narrator recalls how his grandmother comforted him when his father punished him, and then he learns that Kathleen has been standing by since the accident. She comes in to see him briefly, and when he falls asleep, he recalls the first time they made love: He tells her about his concentration camp past and his sufferings, and she tells him that his friends think he is a saint. But in his own mind, he is no saint, and he tries to prove it to her by taking her roughly, without love, even though he feels the presence of his grandmother watching. Later the narrative states that the affair lasted one year and ended in mutual tears.

Next the narrative returns to the hospital as the narrator's condition improves dramatically. Now Kathleen begins her struggle against the death wish in the man she loves. Her strength is the life force within her. She is not used to failure. She is aided by the narrator's friendly doctor, John Russell, who is determined that the narrator, of whom he has grown fond, will get well.

Because the narrator had spoken the name "Sarah" when he was in a coma, Kathleen has had jealous thoughts. Finally she asks the narrator who Sarah is. He informs her that Sarah was his dead mother's name, and that placates her. But we learn that Sarah was also the name of a demented prostitute the narrator had picked up when he was a teenager in Paris. She was a concentration camp survivor who, as a child, had been continually raped by German pedophiles. Her pain drove the desire out of the virginal narrator. He calls her a saint, for to the narrator, those who have endured the unendurable are saints. The narrator fled the girl's apartment and then tried to find her again but to no avail.

The narrative now returns to the days just before the accident, when the narrator had decided that he would have to leave Kathleen once more. The black cloud of his grandmother's memory will not clear and let him try for happiness. But absentmindedly, he agrees to allow Kathleen to try to make him happy by getting him to forget his horrible past. The next day, he had his accident. Ten weeks in plaster casts follow.

A new character enters the narrative: Gyula is a friend and an artist who wants to paint the narrator's portrait. Gyula, a massive life force on the move, takes over the hospital room and orders the narrator to drive the ghosts out of his life and to love Kathleen. The narrator finally realizes that he had seen the taxicab coming and could have avoided the accident. He had really tried to end his life. Now he will try to be happy with Kathleen, but more important perhaps, he is willing to try to bring happiness to her, the woman who loves him so very much. Surprisingly, Gyula burns the portrait he paints of the narrator, but he leaves him with the ashes. The old narrator is dead. The new man rises from the ashes.

SETTING

The Accident is set in the post–World War II milieu that, for Europeans, if not for Americans, was a period of existentialist perception that the world had been torn loose from its supportive anchorage in the universe and was a site of ambiguity and nothingness. But realistic narratives imply a future life for surviving characters, and Wiesel, of course, follows in the tradition. We assume in *The Accident* that the narrator and Kathleen will make a life together, because the narrator has learned that the lie that one is happy not only brings comfort and even happiness to a loved one, but may also bring some peace to the tortured soul of a person whose terrible experiences cannot be expunged fully from consciousness.

The main location in *The Accident* is a hospital room in which the narrator is double-confined in traction and mummylike bandaging. The bandages symbolize his shroud and, progressively, the swaddling cloths of a newborn European child, for the narrator is resurrected, like Lazarus in the New Testament (Fine 1982, 47). The narrator is reluctant to accept "the day." The hospital room is a prison cell for the sufferer, like the basement cell in *Dawn* and, of course, the concentration camp. We modern humans live our lives in cells: apartments, classrooms, offices. Our glimpses of the natural world all too often come to us only through quick glimpses out of windows or in electronically transmitted images.

In *The Accident,* Wiesel employs his characteristic prose, which is lucid, direct, without ornamentation, and easy to read, even if the ideas require the full engagement of mind and heart. Powerful images of chaos and death pervade this dark novel. The narrator walks the city feeling "stunned, heavy, a thick fog in my head" (10). When the narrator was struck down by the cab on a hot summer evening, he dreamed "that I was so cold I was dying. . . . How can one scream against the dying of the light, against life that grows cold?" (17). For him, "Death is not my enemy" (23). His grandmother's ghost, her shawl like a black shroud, floats through the novel. And in the end, symbolic ashes, the ashes of the narrator's earlier life, are left behind when the artist Gyula burns the portrait of the patient in an act of exorcism—driving out the past with its chains and millstones of familial ghosts. Life is renewed, even though the ashes left behind will prevent the narrator from ever being able fully to forget his past. No one fully survives a trauma or a tragedy.

CHARACTER DEVELOPMENT

The narrator is an attractive man about thirty years old who is living in New York City, where he works as a reporter for a foreign newspaper. He is a deeply depressed person, traumatized beyond comprehension to anyone who has not experienced the hell of the German death camps. He is saved from despair and his own death wish by a woman who loves him and by a doctor who loves life. His experiences in the camps tick like time bombs in his psyche; a jarring moment can set one off at any time. The result could be madness or suicide. Kathleen's forceful efforts to get the narrator to commit to a renewed relationship causes his unconscious attempt to take his own life.

In the course of the novel, tortuously, he comes to accept that he has a right to be happy, and that happiness can come from loving and caring for someone else. He turns from being a psychologically wounded and deeply depressed person to a human being with a place in the future. Friendship, love, and the kindness of others may indeed come into one's life, just as horror, tragedy, and catastrophe may also enter.

Kathleen, a proud, beautiful, well-educated woman, born to affluent American parents, has a degree of arrogance because of her privileged place in world society. She has never known suffering until the pain of her difficult, on again, off again, relationship with the narrator. It humbles her, but in the end, she wins her victory—the narrator's willingness to join her in life. She accomplishes this by force of will; not by changing him, but by learning to understand and share his suffering. Even more than the narrator, Kathleen grows emotionally. She has a hard life ahead with her pained lover, but in her mind, and surely in ours, the novel's protagonist is worth the effort.

Dr. John Russell is a physician totally devoted to saving life. This doctor, who has served in the Korean War, has seen enough death. He is at perpetual war with it and will not be defeated. The narrator is his greatest challenge: this man has been critically injured, and he does not seem to want to fight for his life. Russell spends hours in surgery working on the smashed body of the narrator. He fights fever and infection, but he cannot do surgery or prescribe antibiotics to treat a death wish. Perplexed, Russell forces the narrator to tell him his tragic story. That helps both the narrator and the doctor, who realizes that Kathleen's love, loyalty, and willingness to serve are the keys to motivating the narrator to accept life. Russell heals the body and he finds a way to ease the soul.

Sarah, the Jewish prostitute in Paris, appears in only one episode, but her appearance traumatizes both the narrator and the reader. She was maddened by her experience as a twelve-year-old forced to serve as a sex slave to German guards in a concentration camp. After her release, she makes a tormented living in the only trade she knows, selling herself. She reminded the narrator that as terrible as his suffering under the Germans was, some suffered more. As wounded as he is, some are more wounded. The fact that Sarah has the same name as the narrator's mother connects the tormented girl with the narrator's mother, and implies that Jewish men could save neither Jewish mothers nor children. Sarah adds a portion of shame to the narrator's overflowing reservoir of guilt, anger, and depression.

Gyula is a Hungarian artist and a friend of the narrator, who paints the narrator's portrait in the hospital room. He is so strong and domineering that he seems more like a force of nature than a mere human. His function in the novel is to show the narrator that the dead can no longer suffer, only the living can, and that the narrator must think of and care for the living. He provides the exorcism that drives out the dybbuks, the spirits of the dead, from the narrator's mind when he burns the portrait he has completed. Thus he frees the protagonist to live again.

THEMATIC ISSUES

In *The Accident,* Elie Wiesel discusses whether sensitive and aware people could love in the vast killing ground that was the twentieth century. The reader is reminded of the French writer Marguerite Duras's 1961 New Wave film *Hiroshima mon amour,* in which a French woman and a Japanese man struggle to maintain their love in the time after the atomic bomb destroyed the city. Wiesel believes not only that people can find and nurture love in the aftermath of terrible times, but also that they need to, for it is only through a commitment to love that there is the possibility of closing off tormenting memories and enjoying some happiness in the life that is left. As in the French writer Albert Camus's great novel, *The Plague* (1947), a work the French-educated Wiesel must have read early on, Wiesel ends *The Accident* with lovers coming together and with appreciation for the role that close human contacts play in the healing of survivors of catastrophic events.

The Accident pits two primal human motivations against each other: the life force and the death wish. They wage war in the mind of the narrator. The death wish nearly triumphs as the dead haunt him and are ruining his life. But Kathleen and Gyula combine efforts to help him overcome the death of his soul as Dr. Russell helps him keep death from his body.

As an adolescent, Elie Wiesel suffered terribly in concentration camps. Besides the physical suffering, he endured the death of almost all his family at the hands of German murderers. Then, like the narrator in *The Accident,* he suffered a near fatal accident that led to months of pain. It is only natural that Wiesel the philosopher should ask: What is the meaning of suffering? It is an age-old question. The historical answers have been many; the question remains. For Wiesel, suffering does not ennoble the sufferer (Estess 1980, 26); rather, it tends to brutalize. "Suffering," says Wiesel in *The Accident,* "brings out the lowest, the most cowardly in man" (49). What suffering does that is affirmative is give a human being a greater, deeper understanding of life, because suffering is a part of every life. The sufferer must struggle to overcome despair. He or she may need help in doing so. That help may come from faith, but for this narrator, it comes from those who love him, like Kathleen, or those who love human life, like Dr. Russell. Wiesel rejects total acceptance of suffering as a means to a metaphysical end. Rather, he would seem to defy it and in doing so place limits on its impact on one's life (Brown 1983, 225).

ALTERNATE READING: A PSYCHOANALYTIC READING

Psychoanalytic theory is based on the insights and doctrines of Sigmund Freud (1856–1939), an Austrian physician, his disciples, and contemporary reinterpreters. Freud's great contributions were his identification of the unconscious as a major source of psychic energy influencing conscious behavior, and his creation of a model and a vocabulary to explain the psychological sources of human behavior. He saw the mind as having two parts: consciousness and the unconscious. The conscious personality that controls behavior and is in touch with reality Freud called the ego. He called the part of the unconscious associated with instinctive needs and the source of sexual desire the id. It is also a source of psychic energy. What is unacceptable to the conscious mind is stored in the unconscious mind. The part of the mind that holds our conscience, respects authority, and reflects the moral standards of the community is called the superego. Often the superego acts as a brake on the id.

Freudianism has been regenerated in the past twenty years by the work of Jacques Lacan (1901–1981), which emphasizes language as the medium of the unconscious. The machinations of the unconscious, in dreams, for example, can best be understood as enterprises of cultural signification, discourses such as plays, short stories, or novels, all products of language. The inspirational source of the literary work—in fact, all art—is the controlled release from repression of memories that are painful, traumatic, shameful, and always extremely vivid.

Original Freudian theory is criticized in psychological circles today, but contemporary psychoanalytic theory can explain much about the production and the reading of fiction. In studying literature, a psycho-analytic reading could investigate themes of separation or loss. It could discuss the way a character comes to grips with disturbing uncon-scious memories.

In *The Accident,* the narrator suffers from feelings of guilt. He has condemned himself in his unconscious. He feels he has violated his ethical responsibilities to his family in not being able to save it from destruction. Thus his brutal treatment of Kathleen is a result of psy-chological displacement: the transfer of his anger at himself for sur-viving the death of his beloved grandmother and mother onto a living female whom he also loves. Because of his need to punish himself, he has repressed his love for Kathleen, and seemingly has rejected her love for him. The individual is often hardest on him- or herself. The narrator in *The Accident* has judged himself and found himself guilty. The narrative, a confession, is in a sense the evidence in the psycho-logical trial of the narrator and perhaps also of the author. His punish-ments are several and imaginative: One is his inability to find pleasure in life and love; another is his horrifying youthful encounter with the pathetically mad prostitute, Sarah, who, instead of presenting him with his first sexual experience with a woman, evokes taboos and makes him impotent through her horrible tale of multiple rapes by German concentration camp pedophiles. On top of everything else, Sarah shares his mother's name. Most significant, the accident, in the narrator's final introspection, turns out not to have been an accident but a suicide attempt: the narrator was going to punish himself for surviving by joining the dead.

Despair is surely the survivor's disease. It must be brought out, treated, fought, and defeated, or it conquers life itself and achieves the end desired by the torturers. It seems paradoxical to say this, but in a certain sense, Wiesel's concentration camp sojourn was a positive experience, because it gave him his subject for a lifetime of writing, and it gave him a central sustaining purpose to his life: that of pre-serving the memory of the Holocaust dead.

6

The Town beyond the Wall (1964)

The Town beyond the Wall is a post-Holocaust story in which the protagonist, Michael (the name means "who is like God"), a Holocaust survivor, returns to his hometown, Szerencseváro ("city of luck"), twenty years later. In a series of flashbacks, Michael reconstructs his childhood, contrasting it with his tormented present as a prisoner of the communists in Hungary. Writing *The Town beyond the Wall* actually caused Elie Wiesel to visit Sighet, his birthplace, a year after he finished the novel and it was published (1968b, 143–63).

In *The Town beyond the Wall,* Wiesel again discourses on the elusive meaning of suffering. Here, however, he juxtaposes the question with an anatomy of friendship because he sees friendship—valuable beyond measure—as requiring sacrifice and sometimes suffering. Indeed, friendship may be the way to become reconciled to suffering. Significantly, the great friendship in *The Town beyond the Wall* is between a gentile who did not suffer in the concentration camps and a Jew who did. The suffering of Michael under torture contrasts with his previous suffering in the concentration camps in World War II in that the earlier suffering in the Holocaust seems beyond comprehension or understanding, whereas the suffering endured to save a friend has personal and moral significance.

The reviewer Joseph J. Friedman, in the *Saturday Review,* felt that the stories and parables in *The Town beyond the Wall* distract from the plot, and that the novel lacks "narrative pressure." On the other hand, Friedman admired the impressionistic aspects of the novel and the hallucinatory passages. Wiesel shows "genuine talent" (J. Friedman 1964, 26).

PLOT DEVELOPMENT

The narrative begins with Michael, a Jewish boy having frightening childhood experiences in his hometown, which seems much like the youthful Wiesel's Sighet. The boy's father, who appears very early in the story, is much like Wiesel's. After a while, the reader realizes that the early events of the narrative are the recollections and revelations of a man under torture.

The most important event in the narrative of Michael's life is his meeting with Pedro, who becomes not only his friend, but also his teacher. He meets Pedro in Tangier. Pedro is a veteran of the Spanish Civil War (1936–1939), who fought the fascists. With Pedro's help, Michael is smuggled through the Iron Curtain to Szerencseváro, his Hungarian hometown—or what is left of it, because almost all the Jewish people have been murdered. Michael wants to confront a gentile man who watched the rounding up and deportation of the Jewish population in 1944 and did nothing.

The *Town beyond the Wall,* like *The Accident,* has a suspense that comes to closure at the novel's end. The reader wonders why Michael wants to return to Szerencseváro because almost all the other Jews are dead or are far away. He wants to know why gentiles looked on passively, disinterestedly, while the entire Jewish population was deported to death camps. Michael confronts a gentile who watched the deportation and neither did nor said anything. In doing so, Michael confronts moral nihilism, the closing off of one's moral and ethical senses to avoid the unpleasantness of having to imagine the unimaginable.

Unfortunately, shortly after Michael meets the witness and castigates him, the witness informs on him, and the communist police arrest him and put him in prison. There, often delirious while he holds out during three days of interrogation and physical abuse, Michael relates or recalls all the events of his life to his interrogator as he is forced to stand with his face to a wall for twenty-four hours a day, with only a few minutes every eight hours for a visit to a toilet. Then, having saved Pedro's life by not betraying him, Michael is thrown into a cell with other prisoners. We never learn how long he will remain a prisoner or if he ever is released.

Michael has suffered under the Nazis, and now he is suffering under the communists. The police expected that Michael would either "confess" or go mad from the pain in his legs, but he does neither. He will not reveal the smugglers who made the return to his hometown possible. As the novel ends, he resists madness by focusing his life on helping a catatonic prisoner to break his wall of silence, thus bringing him back into the world, and consequently bringing himself to the point of accepting life.

As the interrogation and the torture continue, Michael recalls his boyhood relationship with a very old mystic, Varady, and the young girl, Milika, who took care of the old man. The teenage Michael became infatuated with the beautiful Milika, but their brief romantic relationship was cut off by Michael's deportation.

A later recollection describes Michael's time in a concentration camp, when a beautiful Jewish boy, Yankel, the camp pet of some of the guards, lords it over many inmates. Yankel causes Michael to be horsewhipped. Later, Michael is living in Paris as an impoverished immigrant without a work permit. Yankel, now a young man also living in Paris, tries to make friends with Michael, who resists the friendship because he is depressed, because he has some lingering resentment over how Yankel caused him to be whipped, and because Yankel reminds him that he could not cry when his father died in the camp.

In Paris, Michael also meets Milika again, now a beautiful woman. She is attracted to the handsome young man, and she would like to resume their childhood romance, but Michael rejects that relationship too. He is not ready for love. He feels he is not worthy of it. Indeed, he feels unworthy of life. At the end, of course, by having confronted the indifferent gentile observer, by saving Pedro, by standing up to his torturers, and by aiding a fellow prisoner with a catatonic condition, Michael has earned his own self-respect and is ready to engage life.

SETTING

The Town beyond the Wall is a difficult text to read because of the quick cuts between Michael's past and present, the days under communist torture. The book is divided into sections called Prayers: First, Second, Third, and The Last.

Szerencseváro, Michael's hometown, shares the sad history of much of Eastern Europe in the twentieth century: "First it was a part of

Austria, then it was ceded to Hungary, which gave it to Romania and took it back twenty years later. Then Germans claimed the honor of incorporating it into the Third Reich—which permitted the U.S.S.R. to take it away from her a short time later" (11–12). Most of the forty thousand people of the town never had an allegiance to any of the nations that occupied it.

Of all the locales in the narrative, only Szerencseváro is clearly depicted. Paris is only sketched. Tangier resembles Western views of non-European cultures and places that the critic Edward Said deplores in *Orientalism.* The prison is only vaguely sketched. In fact, the text reads much like an extended parable, although it certainly holds the reader's attention and challenges him or her not to be passive in the face of racist evil.

The wall in the title is, first of all, the wall Michael must face as he is interrogated for three days. But the wall is also a symbol for the despair that encircles Michael like the wall of a town. He must find or build a new town, one without a wall. The new community will be filled with people he cares about and who care about him. It must be a place of living hope. He will begin to build that town when he moves from the interrogation wall and into the prisoners' community in the cell. Perhaps the friendly town without a wall will be the community he will inhabit after the incarceration, if he should survive.

Michael the prisoner must stand while he undergoes long interrogation. Because Hasidic Jews stand when praying, the torture is like praying (Estess 1980, 52). Michael stands for three days of "prayer" under interrogation (is suffering a kind of prayer to God?), and the fourth day of "prayer" is his work of mercy with the mentally disturbed prisoner in the cell (is helping a fellow human a form of prayer?).

The many references to, and images of, legs serve as a leitmotiv and help structure the text. The prayers will break "the toughest legs" (8). Michael tries hard "not to think of my legs" (10). He thinks he "will die on my feet" (20). And he will welcome death "on my feet" (20). Under the torture, he remembers a legend in which God orders Moses to "stretch out your legs" (21). Michael believes that "first my legs will die" (20). A communist interrogator discusses how a prisoner's legs turn into columns under torture (38, 40). Michael thinks that the life of his friend Pedro "is worth a pair of legs" (83). Legs are like spare parts. They are ready to give way when Michael is visiting Yankel in a Paris hospital (88). They can bear him only mechanically as he discusses Yankel's death with a doctor. But Michael's legs never give way.

And finally, Michael thinks his legs have become crutches (98). But Michael's legs symbolize the strong columns of support that prayers provide for those, like Michael, who believe in God, and who follow God's Commandments.

It should be noted that Wiesel's prose style in *The Town beyond the Wall* is staccato and minimalist. One senses that the author wants the reader to pause, to be silent, and to contemplate a journey into and out of a purgatory.

CHARACTER DEVELOPMENT

Michael's ordeal of torture under the communists is the experience that builds his self-understanding and maturity. He needed not only to visit the places of his childhood and youth, but also to confirm the values of his parents and his lost community. Standing at the torture wall stokes his memory and helps him to recognize his own love of life and to codify his compassion. His recollections are the avenue on which he walks to his survival.

Michael's relationship with the mysterious, mentoring Pedro teaches him about loyalty, just as the gentile witness to the deportation of the town's Jews betrayed Michael teaches him about betrayal. He will never betray Pedro, and he will live his life aware that betrayal is one of the ugly and vicious flaws in much of humanity.

For Michael, madness may be a moral choice "as well as a psychological compulsion" (M. Friedman 1978, 211). It can bring comfort in an unbearable situation. It can be an act of free will that destroys freedom. Michael comes close to choosing madness, but in the "Last Prayer," he rejects the easy choice and takes the high road as he fights to save a fellow prisoner who is mentally disturbed. By healing another prisoner, Michael heals himself of guilt, despair, and perhaps loss of faith.

Pedro, the Spaniard, is not only Michael's best friend, he is his teacher. Pedro has inner power, wisdom, and confidence, and he is able to transfer some of these attributes to his younger friend. Pedro is an existentialist. His credo is: "I suffer, therefore I am" (118), and thus he is less interested in stopping suffering than Michael is. Pedro feels that suffering is unstoppable. It is the essential truth and teacher of the human condition. Pedro is willing to live and to create in the face of evil. Michael, on the other hand, wants "to eradicate evil" (Berenbaum 1979, 39). He has "much to learn from the Spaniard" (39). And in the course of the novel, he does learn much.

There is something unworldly about Pedro. He is almost saintlike. It is as if his entire existence is devoted to being an example of righteousness. He puts himself in harm's way, risking torture and death for his disciple, Michael, seemingly only to give Michael the opportunity under torture to overcome the soul-destroying temptation to betray his role model and stop the pain. In doing so, he gives Michael the opportunity to grow into a mensch, a Yiddish term meaning "a truly moral, decent, and compassionate human being."

Varady is an old mystic, slightly mad, who greatly influences Michael in his adolescence. Varady claims to be immortal, but it is only a joke he plays on superstitious people. He sees other men as weak and admires other men only when they, like him, are willing to challenge even the universe. Varady is a hypnotic heretic who believes that humankind is omnipotent. Michael is fascinated by him. The old man kills himself just before he was to be deported to a concentration camp, but his death is kept a secret so the legend of his immortality will survive.

From Varady, Michael learns to detest cowardice. Varady would have Michael do battle even with God. It would seem that Wiesel has invested in the old mystic the very strengths he embraced in his own Hasidic upbringing: the courage to argue with and chastise the God he so fervently believes in, hoping that God will endow the Messiah with necessary human fortitude.

Milika, a beautiful adolescent girl, is Varady's caretaker. She preserves the secret of his mortal death from all but Michael. The young Michael loves her innocently, and Milika cares for him. When they meet in Paris after World War II, she falls deeply in love with him, but it is too soon after his release from a concentration camp and he is not ready for love. Milika is important for the plot because she is the one who, through a man identified as her husband or lover, arranges for Michael to leave Paris for Tangier, where he meets Pedro.

Yankel is a concentration camp survivor like Michael, a person Michael knew in the camp and who desperately wants to make friends with him. Unlike Michael, Yankel, a child in the camp, was treated as a spoiled pet, kept well fed and warmly dressed. He was able to command and mistreat prisoners and even have them punished by the guards. The prisoners despised the child tyrant. So did Michael, especially after Yankel caused him to be whipped. In Paris, Michael rejects the friendship begged for by the desperately lonely young man. Yankel succumbs to a senseless death by being killed by a truck. Yankel's death makes Michael feel guilty for not having forgiven him and accepted friendship from someone so needy and so lonely. Yankel, after all, had lost his father to a German bullet in the neck (56). Michael comes to realize that Yankel deserved both forgiveness and sympathy.

THEMATIC ISSUES

Friendship is a major theme in *The Town beyond the Wall.* Wiesel believes that the greatest possible act of friendship is to save a friend's life. That is what Michael does for Pedro by withstanding three days of torture without revealing Pedro's name and location to the torturers. In the description of the friendship between Michael and Pedro, Wiesel explores "the realms of interdependence" (Berenbaum 1979, 38). He emphasizes the importance of accepting friendship: humans need friends. Michael deeply regrets that he turned down the opportunity of a meaningful, forgiving friendship with Yankel. A life devoted to worship at the expense of human relationships is not what God wants of people. As Pedro said to Michael: "He who thinks about God, forgetting man, runs the risk of mistaking his goal: God may be your next door neighbor" (115). But what is one to do with one's life when all those one cared for are dead? The answer to this despair is to give oneself to the caring of others. In new relationships is new life.

Another important theme in *The Town beyond the Wall* is the importance of accepting moral and ethical responsibility. We are our brother's keeper. One must not be neutral in regard to the suffering of others. The most significant question in *The Town beyond the Wall,* and perhaps in all of Wiesel's literary work, is not why God does nothing about massive suffering, but why most human beings prefer to be spectators rather than protesters when monstrous injustice and cruelty are happening. God may be living or God may be dead, but we are alive. We can act.

Alienation is also a significant theme in *The Town beyond the Wall.* Surely the twentieth century was a century of extended alienation. As Daniel Stern, in the *New York Times Book Review,* points out, many turned to suicide, many went mad, and many found solace in God despite what had happened to them (D. Stern 1964, 14). Stern sees that Michael overcomes his alienation when he suffers for his fellow humans (14). That is a Godlike action, and the way for the tormented young man to find some hope and meaning in the fractured world of post–World War II Europe.

ALTERNATE READING: A PSYCHOANALYTIC READING

For an introduction to psychoanalytic theory, see the alternate reading in the previous chapter.

Written about twenty years after Wiesel was released from Buchenwald concentration camp, *The Town beyond the Wall* functions as a healing mechanism for this survivor and perhaps as a template for healing for other survivors of the Holocaust. Wiesel explores madness in *The Town beyond the Wall*. Psychosis may be a desirable state in the face of horror and cruelty. Illusions and hallucinations can be a desired alternative to an unimaginably terrible reality, such as a concentration camp or a torture room.

Michael needs to expiate his guilt over the fact that when his father was dying, the vicious spoiled child, Yankel, was able to cry at the death of Michael's father, whereas Michael, who truly loved his father, had no tears because his father had become a life-threatening burden to him. The return of Yankel into Michael's life in Paris is unwelcome because Yankel reminds him of his guilt for not mourning the death of his beloved father, a guilt he has repressed. After Yankel is driven away and Michael learns of his meaningless death, Michael's guilt is transferred from the dead father to the dead Yankel. Guilt may destroy motivation for action. In its several manifestations, guilt is a major factor in the deep depression that immobilized Michael from the time of his emancipation from a concentration camp until he returns to Szerencseváro to find out how and why the gentiles of the town could have been so indifferent to the destruction of the Jewish community.

Reconstituting conscience in Hungarian society helps Michael to redeem himself for what his unconscious mind sees as his betrayal of his father. Michael's earlier rejection of Milika's love, something that would have eased his psychological pain and given him some happiness, is due to his unconscious belief that he is unworthy of love. We will never know if Michael, relieved of guilt and engaged in a humanitarian effort, will achieve a life without depression because we never know if he survived the prison and found his "town" beyond the wall.

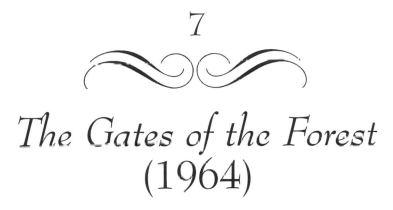

The Gates of the Forest (1964)

In *The Gates of the Forest*, Elie Wiesel once more brings the reader to the terrifying landscape of the Holocaust. The narrative begins in confusion. At first, the protagonist's name is Gregor, a seventeen-year-old Jewish boy living in a cave in a forest after he and his father escaped the deportation of Jews to the German death camps from the Hungarian town in which they lived. His father has left him but has promised to return in three days. It has been many more than three days, however, when the novel opens. Clearly, the father has been captured by the Hungarian police and deported to a death camp where he has been, or will be, murdered.

When a mysterious Jewish stranger appears on the scene, Gregor tells him his name, but the stranger knows that the youth is lying because Gregor is not a Jewish name (12). A few pages later, Gregor reveals that his name is Gavriel but he doesn't use it anymore, so he gives the name to the stranger to use as his own. The Gregor/Gavriel conundrum is solved when one considers that they are a "double" incorporated into a single person, like the young sea captain and his double in Joseph Conrad's famous story, "The Secret Sharer." Indeed, Gavriel may only be a creation of the desperate and frightened Gregor's imagination, just as "the secret sharer" may exist only in the imagination of the insecure captain. But each part of the double manifests an alter ego: the "other." One's fate is what happened, and the other's is what might have happened. But, of course, *The Gates of the Forest* is fiction, the work of the imagination. Its reality is not in the events of a particular life, but in general truths of life.

The significance of the fluidity of names further signifies that the novel is about the loss of identity that accompanied the genocide of Jews. Six million humans were turned into numbers and statistics by the German slaughtering industry.

Like the protagonist Michael in *The Town beyond the Wall,* the protagonist Gregor in *The Gates of the Forest* finds a mentor and friend, a Pedro, whom he names Gavriel. He facilitates Gregor's return to the world he inhabited before the deportations of Jews left only gentiles and the clouds of human dust from the burned bodies in the crematorium that floated back to the lost homes of the Jews. In both *The Town beyond the Wall* and *The Gates of the Forest,* the protagonist experiences a homecoming to a town that has been ravaged by the Holocaust. In *The Gates of the Forest,* however, the protagonist, Gregor, endures the pain of the return and begins to live again.

Unlike protagonists in other Wiesel Holocaust novels, Gregor did not have to endure the inhumanity of the concentration camps (Berenbaum 1979, 53). But he is an Orthodox Jewish youth who has studied the Kabbalah and thus is ready to dispute with the seemingly pitiless God who has betrayed the Chosen People and him. Also, although Gregor endured the trauma of being expelled from the town of his birth, he does not go to his death in Auschwitz like the proverbial lamb to slaughter, but joins the action-filled world of partisan, antifascist fighters. *The Gates of the Forest* is a version of Wiesel's early life as it might have happened if he had not remained with his family waiting for deportation, but had run off to the village home of a gentile family servant and then joined the antifascist guerilla fighters. Perhaps, deep down, Wiesel wished that *The Gates of the Forest* had really been his story.

In a review of *The Gates of the Forest,* David Daiches noted: "It is impossible to discuss Wiesel's novels in the terms which one would normally employ in reviewing fiction. All his works are clearly autobiographical . . . and they represent a genuine and sometimes painful endeavor to come to terms with post-Auschwitz life" (Daiches 1965, 108). John Wain, in the *New York Review of Books,* said that *The Gates of the Forest* is "a neat allegory of the history of the Jews in modern Europe. . . . To say that this is an important book would be an understatement" (Wain 1966, 22–23). Surely, works such as *The*

Gates of the Forest must also be read as documents of modern consciousness as well as works of art.

PLOT DEVELOPMENT

It is the last years of World War II, and a Jewish youth, Gregor, has been hiding in a forest near the town where he and his now dead family had lived. Gregor's father had taken him to a cave in the forest to escape deportation to a death camp with all the other Jews of the town. The father goes for more supplies and never returns. Instead, Gavriel, a mature man, joins Gregor, replaces the father as mentor. He gives his life in order for the youth to have an opportunity to flee to a village where Maria, a kindly Christian and former servant of Gregor's family, shelters and protects him by passing him off as a gentile, the deaf-mute child of her wayward sister.

The terrified Gregor is successful in his lifesaving role as deaf-mute. The people in the town grow fond of him. Because they think he cannot hear or speak, they tell him all kinds of stories of their lives: Men tell him how they lusted for his mother. The village priest confesses that he saved a Jewish man but then threw him out when the Jew refused to be grateful. Captured and tortured, the unnamed Jew, whom Gregor thinks was Gavriel (his alter ego), refused to inform the German authorities that the priest had sheltered him. Consequently, the priest has been tormented by guilt (85).

Finally, the community casts Gregor as Judas in their passion play about the betrayal and crucifixion of Jesus. Playing Judas, Gregor is confronted by a community actor who accuses him of betraying the Son of God. The village actors forget they are in a play. They and the peasant audience cry "betrayal" and try to beat Gregor to death. The attack on the helpless Gregor is a microcosm of every pogrom in Jewish history and even of the Holocaust itself. In his suffering, Gregor realizes that gentiles will always be what they are—persecutors—and he will always be what he is—the Jewish victim (105).

Finally, Gregor cries out. The stunned townspeople think that a miracle has happened and Gregor is a saint. Gregor can no longer bear disguising his Jewishness, and he reveals that he is a Jew. The mob cries "betrayal" again, and attempts to kill Gregor the man, as they had tried to kill Judas the symbol. However, Gregor makes a dramatic but improbable escape with the help of the village mayor, Count Petruskanu, a righteous person, who takes him to another forest where he manages to join a group of resistance fighters.

In the forest, Gregor meets Leib, a childhood friend who had once shown him how to fight off anti-Semitic bullies. He also meets Leib's lover, Clara, a melancholy girl with black hair, and quickly realizes that he will love her one day and stop loving her another day (131–32).

Leib the Lion leads a Jewish resistance group, and Gregor, a messenger now as Gavriel was, brings word to them of what the Hungarians and the Germans are doing to the Jews. Gregor is not fully convinced that Gavriel is dead, and he enlists Leib to help him find out. The search plot goes wrong, and Leib is captured, tortured, and sent to his death. Once more, a friend of Gregor has died for him. Full of guilt, he tries four times to explain to Leib's comrades how their leader was captured. Each time he tells his tale, he implicates himself more deeply because he wants to be punished even though he is innocent of betrayal. He knows that if he had not come to the partisans and told them about the ongoing Holocaust, Leib would still be alive and fighting.

Fortunately, Clara, Leib's heartbroken lover, tells the group to disregard Gregor's statement and to read into his words what is unspoken: that Gregor is meant to be the messenger to the world with the truth of the courage of Leib, a Jewish resistance leader. In the plot to find out if Gavriel is alive and being held in a local prison, Clara and Gregor had to play at being lovers, but he really does love Clara. She, however, is devoted to the memory of her dead hero-lover.

When World War II ends, Gregor, no longer wishing to live in the graveyard that is his native land, goes to Paris, where he meets Clara again. She strongly resists becoming Gregor's lover because of her love for, and loyalty to, the murdered Leib. Gregor wears her down, and they marry. Eventually they move to New York City. The marriage is troubled from the start. Clara is depressed and still thinks about Leib. Though Gregor no longer loves the troubled woman, he is determined to stand by her. Together they will fight off the ghosts of the past who are keeping them from being happy, and they will not worry about the Messiah, who perhaps exists only in the potential for goodness that all people have.

Meanwhile, going into a Hasidic synagogue, Gregor encounters a rabbi who insists that God has not changed since Auschwitz because humans remain able to murder other humans and sacrifice their lives to save others. Still not fully reconciled with God, Gregor finds solace and comfort in Hasidic ritual and the joyous ways of Hasidism through which he is able to reconnect to the religion and the life of his childhood. At the end of the novel, Gregor, led by and by to a synagogue, takes back his Jewish name—Gavriel (224). He has reunited with his double, with his alter ego (Fine 1982, 96). Gavriel is a whole person again.

With each successive narrative, Wiesel honed his fictive skills. He learned to build suspense and shift scenes adroitly. *The Gates of the Forest* is a thought-provoking and satisfying novel.

SETTING

The narrative is divided into four sections: Spring, Summer, Fall, and Winter. In Spring, Wiesel's description of life in the forest refuge is effective and believable. It is the place where Gregor meets and loses Gavriel. The forest is a silent place, but so is the world silent in the face of the Holocaust. In *The Gates of the Forest,* God is silent, perhaps silence itself. At least the forest seems willing to provide cover to those fleeing persecution. This cannot be said for the village to which Gregor, in Summer, runs in order to find shelter with Maria, once his family's servant. There Gregor is silent as the townspeople pour out their innermost thoughts to the youth they believe to be deaf and mute. Then, in fear for his life, Gregor cries out and stuns the crowd. He is chased out of the town like a rabbit running from hounds.

In Autumn, Gregor is back in a silent forest, but Gregor is not silent this time. He is the messenger with terrible tidings, for he must tell the Jewish partisans that all their relatives have been sent to their deaths. The town that Gregor, Clara, and Leib enter to find out if Gavriel is in the prison is a place of deadly danger to Jews. The hatred of the people there for Jews is almost palpable. Gregor hears their vicious words and trembles. It is hell. God is silence there too.

In Winter, many years have passed. Gregor is in New York City, but we have little description or impression of the city. The section, like the season, is short of daylight. Most action takes place either at night or indoors. References to shadows are frequent. The world is cold, partially because it has lost the heat of the bodies of the Jewish dead. Gregor is passing through a night of soul-searching. He talks of the death of his father. And, climactically, he engages in a searing dialogue with a Hasidic rebbe in a synagogue in which the rebbe, after listening to Gregor's indictment of God, asks: "What is there for us to do?" (199). The answer is to live, to act, and to help relieve suffering (Estess 1980, 59). "God awaits us" (201).

CHARACTER DEVELOPMENT

Gregor is a wanderer, a Wandering Jew of the twentieth century. Dispossessed by the German terror, he flees his town with his father, and goes to a forest. Then, after his father disappears, he flees the forest and goes to the village of Maria, the family servant who loves him and who will shelter him. Then he flees the village and takes refuge with Jewish partisans in another forest. Risking entry into a hostile town to try to find his friend Gavriel, he has to flee to the forest once more. Later, he lives in Paris. Then he and Clara go to North Africa, then the Far East, and finally New York City. His itinerary symbolizes the fate, in the last half of the twentieth century, of tens of thousands of Holocaust survivors, a restless people unable or unwilling to return to the graveyards of Eastern Europe, but also unable to escape the past.

Gregor is a person who will never be fully happy in his life. He has suffered too much and has seen too much suffering. His deep disappointment with God embitters his life. When Gregor accepts the silence of the deaf-mute role, he is full of despair. His friend Gavriel has died for him, as his father did. His silence dehumanizes him. When he finally speaks out at a performance of a Christian passion play and terrifies the audience, some hope and an element of manhood return. Despair provokes silence; hope brings speech (D. Stern 1990, 12).

The greatest transition in the life of Gregor is his slow change from protected to protector. When the narrative opens, he has been shepherded to the forest by his father. When his father disappears, Gavriel appears to protect him. Then he goes to Maria, and she protects him. Even the mayor of Maria's village, Count Petruskanu, protects Gregor. In the second forest, Leib is the protector. But when Leib is captured, Clara saves Gregor from execution by the partisans. It is at that point that Gregor comes into manhood. He goes out into the wider world by himself and survives.

Finding Clara again, Gregor urges her to marry him, and when she does, he commits himself to life again, not only to protect Clara as a husband does a wife, but to save her from the demons in her dreams and the ghosts of lost loved ones. As the novel ends, Gregor says of himself: "I've grown . . . I'm older" (220). Experience has given him gravitas. Gregor is a character for whom we not only have sympathy, but also admiration.

Gavriel is a version of the name *Gabriel*. In the Bible, Gabriel is an angel whose name means "man of God," and who intercedes for humans with God. In *The Gates of the Forest,* Gavriel is the older companion to Gregor. For a short time, he becomes a father figure. A strange being, Gavriel seems to have no prior life. He even implies that he is an angel (13). Gavriel laughs persistently and at the oddest moments. The laughter is otherworldly. Gregor blocks his ears at first, for fear that the "other wanted to drive him mad" (21). Gavriel's persistent laughter in the face of calamity, torture, and imminent death is Wiesel's sardonic way of reacting to the great joke that God seems to have played on the Jews: designating them the Chosen People and then subjecting them to two thousand years of persecution and misery.

Gavriel seems fearless; neither the thought of pain nor death frightens him. Gavriel sacrifices his life to save young Gregor, and he does so laughingly. One thinks of him as a supernatural being. He appears from nowhere, as if he were sent by God to save the boy. But Gavriel is a messenger without a message, unless that message is that the father will not come back, and that no one else, including the Messiah, will come for Gregor or any other Jew in peril. Gavriel is a storyteller and, significantly, he tells stories about the coming of the Messiah. But the belief system upon which the Messianic narrative in *The Gates of the Forest* relies is "in the process of collapse" (Davis 1994, 91). Gavriel shows that the Messianic narrative is susceptible to variation and even contradiction (91). In several incidents in Wiesel's early novels of the Holocaust and the immediate aftermath, that narrative is varied, for it is, after all, subject to the circumstances and the intensity of suffering that causes people to cry out for a savior.

Gavriel offers to be Gregor's shadow (40). As long as Gregor possesses a shadow, he is surviving. A person in the grave, or a person turned to ashes, has no shadow. In the dark cave at the beginning of the text, Gregor is unable to distinguish one shadow from another. As the novel progresses, Gregor moves into the light, and into enlightenment, and his shadow—the Gavriel within him—is strong.

Leib, the Lion, is king of the forest, so to speak, but even he is not strong enough to escape the great evil that pervades the human world of the novel. When Leib is captured and deported to a death camp, Gregor feels that he has been Leib's Judas, Leib's betrayer, even though that is not true.

At the end of *The Gates of the Forest,* Gregor, now Gavriel once more, prays for the soul of his friend whom he has come to regard as a role model—a Jewish man of action who is willing to fight those who would kill Jews because they are Jews. Leib is a new Jew, "a warrior," as Gavriel calls him (226). Gavriel considers Leib's immortal quality to be courage. His likes had not been seen since the days of Bar-Kochba, the rebel leader who battled the Romans in Judea in the first century A.D. Gavriel sees Leib as a messenger, not from heaven, but to heaven. The message is that the Jews have become fighters. Never again will they allow themselves to be slaughtered by anti-Semites.

Clara, Leib's lover and later Gregor's wife, is a beautiful girl deeply disturbed by what has happened to her family and her community in the Holocaust. She is hostile to Gregor when she meets him in the partisans' forest bunker, perhaps because she is jealous of his friendship with Leib, a friendship that will cost Leib his life. She cannot love Gregor entirely; Leib still has a powerful hold on her. Wiesel has Gregor believing that love is a victory. It is one way that God works. But Gregor and Clara have no children. She is too wounded psychologically for them to fully possess each other. Although, after years together, Gregor no longer loves his wife, he remains true to his commitment and will stand by her and try to ease her perennial pain. Thus the plot of *The Gates of the Forest* comes to a realistic and satisfactory closure.

THEMATIC ISSUES

A major theme in *The Gates of the Forest* is the search for the answer to the question "How can one believe in God after the Holocaust?" It is a question millions of people around the world asked their religious leaders when, in May 1945, the horror of the German attempt to annihilate the Jews of Europe was revealed. The ultimate answer, as stated by a Hasidic rebbe, is: "How can you *not* believe in God after what has happened?" (194). Not to believe in the Deity is to be left with no anchor in the world and drifting in despair. With hope, one goes on, helps others, gives and accepts love, and lives out one's life. Still, the answer is not fully satisfactory. Wiesel fails "to make his shattering theme—God's betrayal of Man—consistently explicit" (Elman 1996, 5). Much is lost in the opacity of language and construction (Elman 1996, 5).

Humanity's troubled relationship with God is a major theme in *The Gates of the Forest*. In the dark night of his soul, Gregor wrestles with God in the way Jacob wrestled at night with an angel in the Bible.

Gregor wants to "convict God of Murder," as did a court of four rabbis in a concentration camp (197). But they were executed, not God. Gregor seeks to enlist the Hasidic rebbe in New York City to join with him in his protest against God's cruelty, but the rebbe rejects the path of confrontation because it is a manifestation of pride. The rebbe states, however, that if God is malevolent enough to try to take away the reason for singing, the way to defy the Deity is by doing just that: by singing (198). This begins the return to childhood faith for Gregor (Halpern 1978, 77) It is the child in him, the joyfully singing child, who leads the adult man to give God back the "crown and sceptre" in a synagogue (226).

Not surprisingly, the theme of friendship appears again in *The Gates of the Forest.* For Wiesel, the deepest friendship occurs when one friend is so close to the other that they seem to become one. Gavriel becomes Gregor, who is really Gavriel. Gregor becomes Leib in the mind of Clara. But even less intense friendships are not only of value in life, but very necessary for life.

It is a friendship with an office colleague, Mandel, first avoided by Gregor, that leads him back to the joys and comforts of Hasidism (195). Gregor had said to Mandel: "I stay away from friendship. It's too noisy" (195). He still preferred silence and even loneliness. But as friendship grew, Mandel helped Gregor to reveal his happy childhood, and it is Mendel who sees that a return to a religious dialogue could be the way for Gregor to alleviate his pain

ALTERNATE READING: A FORMALIST READING

In mid-twentieth-century America, Formalism was the major school of literary criticism. Associated with the critical group called the New Critics, and referred to as New Criticism, it proposed a simple but revolutionary theory: the understanding of the work of literature, and what that work was about, resided in its form. Artistic technique was more significant than subject matter. The way to understand the work was through its construction. The form of the work is an essential part of its content. Almost all readers begin to interpret a work of literature by becoming aware of the way form relates to the tone, action, and meaning of the text. Some formalists insist that content, meaning, and significance are merely aspects of form.

Formalists objectify the work of literature and valorize it as an object. The text's qualities are a result of craft. Artistic judgment and choice are matters for consideration in evaluating the use of language, imagery, and, most of all, symbol: in other words, the employment of the raw materials of wordsmiths. The writer's life, the milieu of composition, the social significance of the work, and the moral and ethical implications of the text are all considered extraneous.

It should be noted that Russian Formalism, a school of literary criticism that evolved early in the twentieth century, focuses on language and tends to disregard content. Russian formalists are intrigued by these questions: How is literary language different from ordinary language? and What are the literary devices employed to create literary language?

From a modern formalist or new critical perspective, *The Gates of the Forest* is an exciting book with some flaws. The tension in the narrative is carefully constructed and very effective. The reader worries about Gregor's fate as the Hungarian Jew hunters are looking for him in the forest after Gavriel has inadvertently revealed to the perfidious villagers that a Jew is in the forest. Also, the reader is held in suspense as to whether Gregor's lifesaving disguise as a deaf-mute will hold. Symbols abound: The forests—nature's domicile—are places of refuge, whereas the towns—human habitats—are places of hatred, betrayal, and murder. The Christian passion play, through which the peasantry is whipped up to violence even against a mere actor playing Judas, stands for Europe's insane history of pogroms.

The weaknesses of *The Gates of the Forest* include the continual storytelling that sometimes stretches the tension of the plot, but often digresses, and seems only to extend a rather slim narrative. The confusion over the names *Gregor* and *Gavriel* weakens the structure of the narrative, as does the long episode late in the text when Gregor tells his companions how their leader, Leib, was captured by the Hungarian fascists. He gives them five versions of the events and finally turns to Clara to give the facts and exonerate Gregor (174).

Wiesel makes a careless mistake in the text: In the beginning, we are told that Gregor's father has left him in the forest. He never actually learns how and when his father died. At the end of the narrative, however, Gregor remembers the anniversary of his father's death and that his father had died in Buchenwald concentration camp "on a wooden bed" (223) where the old man called out to God in his last words. This, of course, is how Eliezer's (in *Night*—and presumably Wiesel's) father had died. The source of the information is not mentioned, and it seems unlikely that a witness would have survived Buchenwald, found Gregor somewhere in the world, and, from the harvest of death, remembered the time, place, and last words of just one victim.

But, all aspects considered, *The Gates of the Forest* has an organic unity based on Gregor's struggles that sustains the reader's interest.

Part III

After the Holocaust: Hope and Despair

8

A Beggar in Jerusalem
(1970)

The "central paradox of the literature of the Holocaust [is that] it cannot embellish on history" (Langer 1978, 47). The awful power of the Holocaust sets limits on the imagination. It prevents the reader from accepting an invented reality that in any way strays from the brutal historical facts. With *A Beggar in Jerusalem*, Wiesel, developing as a novelist and aging as a person, begins to distance himself and his work from the most traumatic and formative event in his life. Yet he cannot abandon the Holocaust; it is a part of him. But he can move it to a less prominent position in his work. In *A Beggar in Jerusalem*, Wiesel explores much more fully than he did in *Dawn* the relationship between the Holocaust and the founding of the modern Jewish state: Israel (Des Pres 1978, 50). But although time moves on and locales change, many Wiesel themes remain in the foreground.

A Beggar in Jerusalem is another Wiesel novel about the necessity of starting over even after disaster and loss of hope. World Jewry, in a sense, started over after the Holocaust by building Israel. In the beginning, the protagonist again fights "against the forces of ending" (Estess 1980, 63). Elie Wiesel chooses as the background for this story of renewal the 1967 Six-Day War between Israel and the Arab world, the epic struggle for survival that culminated in what seemed to people everywhere a miraculous victory for the nineteen-year-old Jewish state. It was a victory that first appeared to the world as impossible.

"Like others hurt by the sharp edge of anti-Semitism, Wiesel was drawn to Zionism from the first" (Kahn 1990, 109). The thought of a Jewish homeland that could be a refuge for Jews anytime was and is comforting to a people who, when faced with extermination, found the borders of almost every country in the world closed to them. "Only Wiesel . . . has been capable of uniting the holocaust and the emergence and survival of the state of Israel without denying the mystery or reality of either or turning one into historical cause and the other into historical effect" (M. Friedman 1978, 219).

V. S. Pritchett, in the *New York Review of Books,* says that *A Beggar in Jerusalem* "is a story of great tragic power" (Pritchett 1970, 12). But basically it is a story of deep friendship. David and Katriel are such good friends that they seem like one person, something that Katriel's wife, Malka, immediately recognizes. Katriel dies in battle against the Arabs, although his body is never found. David lives on. He is the beggar of Jerusalem, seeking not alms, but listeners to hear his story and validate both his existence and that of Katriel.

PLOT DEVELOPMENT

The plot of *A Beggar in Jerusalem* depicts the struggle of David, the narrator, to comprehend the meaning of his life as it has unfolded in, and been affected by, two great historical events of the twentieth century: the Holocaust and the birth of the State of Israel. The story depicts a deep friendship between David, a Holocaust survivor, and Katriel, a Talmud teacher and a reserve soldier. In the beginning of the narrative, after the Six-Day War in which Israel made Jerusalem once more the capital of a Jewish country, David shares stories with other "beggars" or storytellers at the foot of what for centuries was called the Wailing Wall (now referred to as the Western Wall)—a remnant of the Second Temple where for centuries, Jews prayed for the return to Jerusalem of all Jewish exiles and for the coming of the Messiah to redeem them. He offers accounts of his childhood in Europe, his experience in the concentration camps, his post–World War II life as a broken survivor, and the trauma of his return to the town of his birth: in other words, the subjects of all of Wiesel's previous novels. Also, as in Wiesel's previous novels, the author uses flashbacks to fill in the background to the present moment when David is telling his story.

Katriel has disappeared, and it is presumed that he died in the fierce battle to liberate the Holy City. Cutting back to just before the battle for Jerusalem, the narrative depicts the last time David and Katriel are together. David is not a soldier, but he insists upon going into combat when the war of survival begins. He has survived the Holocaust, but he does not want to survive the seemingly assured destruction of the Jewish state and the death of untold Jews. David is sure of his death the next day in battle, and wonders why that death will come "in this land?" Is it because he is Jewish and forty years old? Is it because he is tired of running from the dead? (163) Ironically, despite his death wish, David is doomed to survive. Israel is saved, but survival is a burden.

The climax of the novel takes place when the victorious Israeli army fights its way through Jerusalem to take the Western Wall (190–98). In that heady moment, the city exists on both a temporal level and a spiritual one. On the former, the soldiers and Israeli citizens rejoice at the restoration of the Jewish capital. On the latter, the hosts of heaven and the souls of all the Jews who have died in exile over the past two millennia join in the Jubilee, for they too are part of the triumph.

David finds it unbearable to contemplate, let alone accept, that his friend is gone forever. He marries Malka, Katriel's widow, and loses his identity as it merges with that of his dead friend. Now he lives to tell his story at the Western Wall and to be taken care of by his understanding wife, whose love for her dead husband and love for her living husband are one and the same.

In the end, David is not even sure of Katriel's name. Katriel is a part of David, and yet he also seems almost a part of the Deity, whose magical name, traditionally, is lost or at least beyond utterance (205). He thinks, or merely hopes, that Katriel will come back someday, perhaps with a different name, and David will tell the mysterious returnee of Katriel's adventures, thus reconstituting his life (206).

Ultimately, the beggar of Jerusalem must be Wiesel himself (Fine 1982, 108): He is the storyteller, he is the witness who keeps alive the memory of those made nameless by the Germans and their fascist allies, he works in both the oral and the written traditions. And he is a creator, a literary artist, who breathes life into history through his fictive skills. Katriel's last words to David before he vanishes are: "You must write something new" (195).

SETTING

Wiesel employs a narrator-protagonist in *A Beggar in Jerusalem*. David is yet another Wiesel protagonist-survivor whose early history parallels the author's. David, having endured so much as a youth and having seen his family destroyed, does not want his life to end in the same way that he does not want the life of the Jewish people to end: Hitler's goal. David is named after King David of the Bible, of course, and he is now in Jerusalem, the City of David, the first Israelite king of the Holy City.

The Western (Wailing) Wall is the main symbol of *A Beggar in Jerusalem.* It is "the source from which the collective memory of the Jewish people emanates" (Fine 1982, 105). It is a major symbol of Jewish history, a wall that unifies instead of dividing. It brings together living Jews and the spirits of the six million Holocaust dead, who, in a sense, gave their lives so that the Wall could once more stand in the center of Jewish religious and secular life. All the characters in *A Beggar in Jerusalem* are touched by the Wall, which in its liberation becomes a place now for exultation, not mourning.

Perhaps the most brilliant aspect of *A Beggar in Jerusalem* is the description of the Holy City in 1967 as seen through the eyes of a survivor of the German death camps. Wiesel is also skillful in his description of the capture of the Old City of Jerusalem during the Six-Day War. He shows the event through the impressions of a civilian, David, who enters the conflict to be near his friend, to experience a great and redemptive moment in Jewish history, and perhaps to die in a moment of Jewish exaltation two millennia in the coming.

Brilliantly, Wiesel depicts the fighting ascent of the Israeli army to the Temple Mount, where is the epiphany of modern Jewish history, Jews witnessed "the rejoining of the Western Wall to the heart of Israel" (Leviant 1970, 27).

CHARACTER DEVELOPMENT

David is a forty-year-old Jewish survivor of the Holocaust. He has come to Jerusalem because it is a haven for the remnants of post–World War II European Jewry. He has found a deep friendship with Katriel, whom he cares for more than he cares for himself; indeed, he has come to think of his friend as his alter ego. Although a civilian, David goes into the battle for Jerusalem to be near Katriel. David fully expects to die in the coming attack, perhaps as a sacrifice so Katriel may live, remain married, and have a child to replace the one who died. David thinks that he is the individual without a future. Katriel is

David's obsession, his "private madness. I may even have invented him" (34). Katriel is David's "Other" and the heroic man he would have liked to have been. Katriel is also David's shadow. When Katriel disappears in battle, David and "his shadow will finally become one, just as the ancient people and young Israeli nation may become one" (Sperber 1970, 34).

Katriel (the crown of God) is a Sabra, a native-born Israeli and a Talmudic scholar, but like Leib in *The Gates of the Forest*, he is also a Jewish warrior, this time fighting not the anti-Semitic Germans and their allies, but the Arab nations determined to destroy the fledgling Jewish state in the Six-Day War. Katriel represents Wiesel's belief that both religious and secular Jews must be prepared to defend themselves from those who hate them, those infected with the two-thousand-year plague called anti-Semitism, so that never again will Jews be herded into death camps and slaughtered like sheep when irrational hatred seizes the mind of a nation.

At the same time, Wiesel insists on the basic humanity of Katriel. He is a reluctant warrior, as, perhaps, every warrior should be. He does not want to kill. He does not enjoy killing. He is more "a man of peace and probity who fears being afraid" (Pritchett 1970, 12). Katriel deserved to live, to go back to his wife and to his teaching, and that is why David lives Katriel's unfinished life for him and tells his story.

Malka is a beautiful and loving woman, but she is also another sad, depressed Wiesel heroine. She and Katriel lost their child to illness. She does not want her loving husband to go to war, but he must. It is his sacred duty. She has premonitions of his death. In becoming David's wife, she participates in David's plan to fulfill his friend's unfinished life. Malka is a woman who, unfortunately, was not made to be happy. She knows that the way to fight death is to create life, but she seems destined not to bring new life to the Jewish people.

Lieutenant Colonel Gad is a courageous combat leader in the Israeli army and the officer in charge of the final attack on the Old City of Jerusalem. He is a former friend of David, from the days immediately after the end of World War II when they were schoolmates in France. David had come from the death camps, but Gad was a Palestinian Jew. As the 1967 Arab-Israeli war approaches, David, wanting to witness the battle for Jerusalem and to be near Katriel, cajoles Gad into letting him accompany the army in the assault. Sadly, the courageous Gad, like Katriel, dies in the battle. He is another "new" Jew, a warrior.

THEMATIC ISSUES

The theme of the witness is of paramount importance in *A Beggar in Jerusalem*. David the storyteller, like Wiesel, is a witness who must keep alive the memory of dead Jews. He has a desperate need to avoid finality, and he also needs a possible witness who will survive him and testify that he existed (Fine 1980, 102). His solution is the formation of a double with Katriel (like the relationship between Gregor and Gavriel in *The Gates of the Forest*). The survivor will be both persons in one. David fully expects to be the one to die first. He projects no life beyond his imminent death in battle. Therefore, when he survives, he must live more for Katriel than for himself. His life must be a living memorial to his other being, because the burden of the survivor is to keep the dead "alive."

Related to the theme of the witness is that of the presence of the absent. This is a theme that transcends much of the work of Elie Wiesel. Orthodox Jews believe that a person lives on if his or her name lives on in a descendant, and therefore, both spiritually and biologically (through genes), the dead are present. So the Holocaust dead—the absent—make their presence known in art, language, historical writing, museums, and literary monuments.

A mystical theme in *A Beggar in Jerusalem* is the possible relationship between God's will and the creation of the Jewish state. The juxtaposition of the satanic acts of Adolf Hitler and his German henchmen in their twelve-year reign of terror and the "return" of hundreds of thousands of Jews to the Holy Land—as in biblical and talmudic prophecy—from all over the planet within three years of the demon's suicide stunned not only world Jewry but thoughtful Christians everywhere. Simply put, Wiesel, the angry believer, is sure that the gift of the Return was God's penance for allowing the Holocaust. Jerusalem once more is central to "the memory of an entire people" (202).

In *A Beggar in Jerusalem,* Wiesel takes pains to exonerate millions of Jews of complicity in the Holocaust because "they let themselves be massacred, like saints perhaps, but not like men" (112). Wiesel indicts the world: "By going to their death, the victims showed the world that it judged itself unworthy of either salvation or destruction; no living person has the right to hold that against them" (112).

ALTERNATE READING: A NEOPRAGMATISM READING

Neopragmatism as a critical theory is based on the writings of John Dewey, the great American philosophical pragmatist of the late nineteenth and early twentieth centuries. Pragmatism argues against finding metaphysical significance, such as spiritual insights or even the source of ultimate reality, in mere philosophical thought and intellectual exercises. It argues, pragmatically, against theoretical conjecture, and for locating truth through experiment, discovery, and practical employment. Theorems should be judged by practical results.

Neopragmatism argues that the novel is very useful because it provides a better way than any other medium of understanding the world. In fact, the novel creates of itself a real world open to interpretive reading through which an unlimited number of human voices, perspectives, and values may be presented by the author or derived by the reader. The literary text and the pragmatic criticism of the text provide a more satisfactory tool for living than any traditional philosophy or other critical theories that focus on "literariness."

A Beggar in Jerusalem is a useful book in many ways. In re-creating life in the Jewish section of divided Jerusalem before the 1967 war, Wiesel shows the reading public how desperate the two million Israeli Jews were when they found themselves faced with the enmity and threatened violence of 100 million Arabs. He makes clear the reasons why almost all the people of Europe and the Americas sympathized with their plight, coming as it did only a generation after the attempted genocide of the Jewish people. The Israeli triumph seemed a miracle not only to Jews but to many Christians who believed that the return of the Jews to the Holy Land preceded, according to prophecy, the future second coming of Jesus Christ.

The narrative also explains why Jews almost universally believe that Israel, the Holy Land, is their country even though they live elsewhere. The Right of Return to Israel was bought with the blood of the Six Million and the blood of the Jews who fought to save the young country created and sanctioned by the United Nations after World War II. In *A Beggar in Jerusalem,* Wiesel helps to make true (ideologically speaking, truth is what a community decides is truth) the right of the Jewish people to return to the land God promised them. *A Beggar in*

Jerusalem "is an ambitious attempt to show how Jewish spirit and ideology brought victory in June 1967" (Leviant 1970, 27).

Ultimately, *A Beggar in Jerusalem* creates an interesting and vibrant world for the reader to explore. The text, like all literary texts, is ultimately about itself. It is a work in, and of, language. The reality of the world it portrays is a matter of words. The understanding of life and its meaning that we derive from *A Beggar in Jerusalem* are located in the imagination. Understanding and meaning come into existence in the process of reading.

9

The Oath
(1973)

In *The Oath*, Elie Wiesel affirms that the thinking and feeling person must move beyond contemplating the great questions of life and take action. One must not wait for answers that may never come. Knowing, feeling, and acting on the questions suffice. A great question for Wiesel, for Jews, and for the world is: What is the meaning of the Holocaust? Wiesel now lays that question aside in *The Oath*, and he concentrates on how Jews—and, by extension, all human beings—can exist in a post-Holocaust world; for surely, Auschwitz destroyed most of the basic assumptions about the presence of God, the goodness of humankind, and the moral progress of civilization. Now the burden of existence falls not on the survivors of genocide but on those born after the terror. The post-Holocaust world seems both exhausted and absurd. Looking back on the Holocaust in *The Oath*, Wiesel sees only insanity. Writing about *The Oath* in the *New York Times Book Review*, Alan Friedman said that "At his best Elie Wiesel is a remarkable fabulist whose vision can transform slaughter into farce and back again" (A. Friedman 1973, 5).

For Wiesel, the key to human survival now is for all people not to give in to despair but to embrace life. Sorrow is a contagious disease. If we live for others, our sorrow diminishes, and in that way, we live for ourselves. The post-Holocaust world is a world stunned, shaken, and rudderless. In commitment, we may find purpose and peace, if not happiness. In *The Oath,* the saving of just one life is a blessing on the person who does it and a gift to the person who is saved.

PLOT DEVELOPMENT

The opening action in Part 1 of *The Oath,* entitled The Old Man and the Child, takes place in an unnamed city in the late 1960s or a little later. An unnamed young man is present. The indefinite person, place, and time serve Wiesel's intention to have the narrative stand for the universal. The story is about an encounter between generations. At one end is the young man who is contemplating suicide and who is essentially alone in the world. He has endured many vicissitudes and has retreated to reflect on the purpose and value of life. At the other end is an old man, Azriel, the narrator, who believes that political and social activism is the way to help humankind and, simultaneously, make life meaningful for the individual. He wants to prevent the young man from killing himself. He continually engages the young man in conversation, forcing the youth to talk, knowing that "One does not commit suicide in the middle of a sentence" (14).

Azriel has taken a strange oath not to talk about a terrible event in his youth, the pogrom that forty years ago caused the death of all but one of the inhabitants of his native Hungarian village, Kolvillàg. (*Kol* is Hebrew for "every," and *villàg* is Hungarian for "village." Fused together, the word now signifies the entire world.) Azriel was the only survivor. In the course of the narrative, he gives succeeding hints about the event and, in the end, reveals all.

In Part 2 of *The Oath,* entitled The Child and the Madman, and Part 3, entitled The Madman and the Book, the novel moves away from the flashbacks, prose-poetry, and stream-of-consciousness passages to a more direct and realistic narrative. Azriel, the sole survivor of the pogrom in Kolvillàg, slowly proceeds to inform the reader of the brutal destruction of his village. The inciting event of the massacre is the disappearance of a Christian youth. A stable boy has disappeared with some of his father's horses; he is neither liked nor missed, not even by his parents. Nevertheless, the Jews of the town are accused of ritual slaughter of a Christian, an ancient, irrational slander of the Jews and an excuse for rape, robbery, and murder from the Middle Ages to the twentieth century. Actually, the boy is alive, and he reappears in the pogrom at the story's end.

As tensions mount, and a pogrom seems inevitable, Moshe, a mad mystic who is Azriel's teacher, offers to confess to the crime he did not commit and that in fact did not happen, in order to save the Jewish community from sure death. But they are not saved. Moshe is wrongly imprisoned by the authorities for the murder of the Christian boy. He is horribly tortured, but he steadfastly holds to his faith in God.

Given permission to make a public address at the synagogue, Moshe persuades the Jews of Kolvillàg to take a vow that if anyone happens to survive the inevitable pogrom, that person will never speak of the destruction of the town. Moshe is a new Moses, and his commandment is silence. "If suffering and memory are intrinsically linked then the former can be destroyed by attacking the latter" (Berenbaum 1979, 93). Moshe is wrong, of course: Memory is powerful. Powerlessness does not prevent persecution; it invites it. Silence and genocide go hand in hand. The pogrom occurs, and ironically the fires that are started by the rampaging Christians burn down the entire town too.

In Part 2, the Jews of Kolvillàg desperately appeal to officials and the local nobility for action to prevent the incipient pogrom as mindless Christian hatred grows out of control. Their appeal is unanswered. Officialdom turns a blind eye to the obvious, and hides behind its professed belief that Christians are civilized people who would never attack the Jewish community. Part 3 depicts in graphic detail the long-awaited massacre and the surprising destruction of the town by fire when the pogrom gets out of hand.

But Azriel has kept the oath until the needs of the young man conflict with Azriel's loyalty to the dead. Breaking the oath and narrating the unspeakable permit Azriel to offer the young man a reason for living: essentially to replace the missing and to preserve their story. The young man's suicide would be another murder, another killing in the long history of the slaughter of Jews, and thus "only a gift to death" (E. Stern 1982, 178). What Azriel achieves in relating the life and death of Kolvillàg is the gift of a community to the young man. He now has a past he can comprehend. He now has a mission: remembering.

Although the Jewish community of Kolvillàg is destroyed despite the efforts of Moshe, it can be rebuilt in another time and place through and in the memory of the living and the dedication of living Jews to live out their lives, passing Jewish memory on to future generations. In a theological sense, the Jews are God's memory. Death of a community or an individual has nothing to recommend it. People must move beyond despair even if life is not as beautiful as it seems in some films.

Saved from the burning ruins of the village is the communal archive, the *Pinkas,* a sacred relic of the community, given to Azriel by his father, Shmuel, who is the town scribe. The *Pinkas* was started in 1851, and is a history of confrontation with gentile hatred and violence. That document, sealed by the oath of silence, is the key to the resurrection of the Jewish community, for ultimately it is through the written word that a people and an individual writer bear witness. Language, after all, is a "means of survival" (Fine 1982, 110). In a way, Wiesel, as author of *The Oath,* is the last writer in the *Pinkas* (Lamont 1990, 135).

As a novel, *The Oath* does have some problems, such as an occasional character cliché and too many passages of bookish rhetoric passing for philosophy (Wood 1974, 12). But the power and the truths of the novel override all shortcomings.

SETTING

In the end, Wiesel chose in *The Oath* to write about the Holocaust by not writing about the Holocaust. The very vastness and complexity of the Holocaust precludes writing it as a single story. So Wiesel uses the destruction of Kolvillàg in 1920 as a microcosm and a foreshadowing of the Holocaust to come (Davis 1994, 103).

Although the anonymous city that is the setting for the narration in *The Oath* is vaguely described in order to stress its universality, Kolvillàg is fully and richly depicted. The Balkan coarseness and corruption of the village in the Carpathian Mountains is portrayed in exquisite detail. We see the mendacity of the hierarchy, the drunken cruelty of the peasants, the impotence of the church, the tendency of the Jewish community to deny the danger they are in because they cannot bear to contemplate what will happen to them. Their denial is because they have no place to run to, and because, except for a handful of brave youths ready to fight, they have done little or nothing to defend themselves despite the long history of hatred and violence against them in the region.

In Part 3, the attack on the Jewish community is so vividly portrayed by Wiesel that the reader envisions a version of the Apocalypse where madness, rage, drunkenness, cruelty, sadism, bestiality, slaughter, horror, and terror have inundated the world. The town catches fire almost as if angry angels have put a torch to it. Everything burns. All are killed except Azriel. The meaning of the total destruction of Kolvillàg is simply that hatred destroys both the hater and the hated. This section of *The Oath* illustrates Wiesel's considerable narrative skills.

A major symbol in *The Oath* is the chronicle of Jewish Kolvillàg, the *Pinkas*. It is sacred to the community because it contains the community's history, just as the Hebrew Bible contains the history of the Jewish people. The community's greatest fear is not the loss of their lives but the loss of the *Pinkas* (177). It symbolizes the regard Jews have for all their holy books, the Torah, the Talmud, the very scrolls in the countless Arks. They must not be desecrated or be lost to humankind.

By the time Wiesel wrote *The Oath*, he had established a signature, an autobiographically informed narrative in which a young, Jewish, male survivor of the Holocaust who has lost his family and community, and who lives through a period of hardship as a stateless person, either returns to his original homeland to seek understanding or finds a new homeland in Israel. *The Oath* differs from this formula in that the terrible pogrom takes place some twenty-five years before the genocide that the Germans attempted on the Jews of Europe.

The Oath is, of course, an aesthetic composition. Part 1 is replete with enigmas and obscurities, whereas Parts 2 and 3 are consciously juxtapositional to Part 1 because of Wiesel's decision to revert to chronological narration. The operative tension of the novel is Azriel's struggle against the of oath of silence that binds him as he seeks ways, like Scheherazade, to use a story to keep a life alive: the life of a young man. For Wiesel, "Death has no meaning. It is useless" (189).

CHARACTER DEVELOPMENT

The young man is the son of a woman who survived the death camps in which she had lost a previous child. She has implanted her memories of the horror into her son, and thus she has deprived him of a full and happy life. She is unable to see her son as he is and understand him, because every time she looks at him, she sees in him the lost others. The young man's childhood has harmed him greatly, because, although not a survivor of the concentration and death camps, he lives the horrors in his mind. As a result, he is deeply depressed. Life holds no joy for him. It is as if the murdered dead of Europe are calling him to join their ranks. Thus suicide, so alien to Jewish values, seems to be to him a viable way to ease his psychological suffering.

Wiesel is making a significant point: children of survivors of the Nazi Holocaust—indeed, children of survivors of any genocide—may share the post-traumatic stress of their parents. In part, this was and is why many Holocaust survivors did not want to tell their children what had happened to them.

Azriel is an old man, nearly eighty, who survived a pogrom that killed all the people, Jews and gentiles, of his Eastern European village, Kolvillàg, early in the twentieth century and long before the mid-century Holocaust. But the village slaughter is Azriel's Holocaust. He is part madman and part saint. He stands for every man, for all people facing the possibility of extermination because of race, religion, or even nationality in a world perpetually brimming over with hate. Azriel must find a meaning for his life, and in old age, he does. He is meant to save the life of the young man, and in doing so, save the Jewish people. He realizes that the young man, in allowing Azriel to enter and to save his life, has given meaning to Azriel's life. Thus Azriel defeats death.

Moshe is a truly mad but saintly mystic. He thinks that by not speaking, that is, by not employing language, he can stop history. The young man's idea of despising the present world and retreating from life is also endorsed by Moshe, who believes that this world is not beautiful to behold. The spiritual world, the world we carry inside us, is the preferable one.

John K. Roth points out that Moshe believes that the Jewish people do not believe in martyrdom (Roth 1978, 70). Moshe says that Jews "consider death the primary defect and injustice inherent in creation. To die for God is to die against God" (189). Moshe wants to shame God through silence, to reach God's heart by rejecting the Creator's gift of language that forms the prayers that God expects and requires.

Ultimately, Moshe's gift to Azriel is a life-preserving blessing. He said, and Azriel remembers: "May God save you not from suffering but from indifference to suffering" (87).

Shmuel, Azriel's father, is important to the narrative in that he, as the community scribe, is able to pass on to his son the records of the Jewish community of Kolvillàg, thus saving their story and keeping alive the memory of the murdered Jews. The *Pinkas* is the monument to Kolvillàg. Always, the written word and the religious book are deeply revered by the Jewish people and are seen as vital to their survival as a people.

THEMATIC ISSUES

A major theme of *The Oath* is the debate between ideological activism—taking political action in accordance with one's convictions—and philosophical retreat—avoiding political action through continuing deliberation. Which position affects world memory more? Wiesel does not want the world ever to forget what happened to European Jews from 1933 to 1945. He sees merit in both of the preceding positions. Old Azriel, like the author, has been a person with a social conscience. He has worked to help the poor and alleviate human suffering. He is desperately trying to save the young man from suicide. Yet Azriel is also dedicated to preserving and passing on the book of Jewish memory. That is one key to Jewish survival: the reverence for the book. To write the history of terrible times and even great defeats is, in a way, finally to win by validating survival. In a theological sense, the monotheistic God—in Christianity, Islam, and Judaism—is a Jewish God after all, creating history and demanding that it be recorded. Wiesel is sure that the Jews are God's memory, and that memory is preserved in Judaism.

A second significant theme in *The Oath* is the idea that any encounter between two human beings changes the individuals and the world. Indeed, such an encounter is like the collision of particles that changes an unstable atom and sets off a chain reaction. Azriel believes that his encounter with the young man is the reason for his existence because it presented him with the opportunity to "defeat death in this particular case" (32). In saving one young person from suicide, one saves the world. Wiesel, perhaps because he has seen so much death, is passionately for life. Also, Wiesel implies in *The Oath* that we create and reveal our individual character out of "those countless deeds that we unthinkingly undertake or fail to undertake on behalf of other persons" (Estess 1980, 94). On the other hand, the specific and memorable moments of our lives, the actions we take after deep thought, are not necessarily the foundations of self.

Third, *The Oath* discourses on the nature of language. Wiesel sees language as ambiguous and even treacherous because it can be employed by the unscrupulous to change what has really happened. It is more protean than putty. Furthermore, language is inadequate to describe experience. Sometimes it is better to avoid language. Wiesel has long been interested in silence. He was silent about his experiences in the death camps for ten years after his release. Moshe, the madman in *The Oath,* is wary of language because he believes it helps create the terrible reality his community faces. Not speaking of danger may cause it to go away. This, of course, is madness. But the Jews have tried everything else in their long history of trying to avoid injustice, cruelty, and murder, and everything else has failed. Perhaps silence might prove efficacious? Perhaps silence will put an end to history? Moshe's idea of sacrificing God's gift of language to appease the Deity is of no avail. However, the community vow not to speak of the pogrom if any survive is futile. Hatred and murder will be served. The Jews have been called the People of the Book. Their great gift to humanity has been the Bible. But surely the world has not thanked them for their words.

ALTERNATE READING: A DECONSTRUCTIONIST READING

Deconstruction, sometimes called poststructuralism, is an analytical tool devised in the 1960s by Jacques Derrida, the French philosopher who coined the critical term. It focuses on the use of language in critical analysis, and insists that a fictional narrative does not refer to a hard and singular reality outside the text but may have several possible meanings. Also, a narrative may refer to or be based more on other texts than on real life. In other words, there is really nothing outside the text. Deconstruction asks readers to be skeptical of critical readings that provide indisputable meanings, especially those that endorse hierarchies such as men over women or Western over Third World.

Deconstruction exposes and subverts unarticulated presumptions that underlie narratives and often reflect the values of whatever political or economic force is dominant at the time of composition. In other words, a deconstructionist reading tells us what consciously or unconsciously motivated the author to write the book as he or she did. Furthermore, novels are not life. Words are words, not what they represent; the association of words with things is arbitrary. Readers understand words differently. What the words actually say may depend on context, milieu, or history. And what they say differs with individuals. In a sense, we are always translating what we read into the language of our mind. In the end, words are principally uncertain. After all, when we look into a dictionary to find the meaning of a word, all we find are other words.

The individual reading of the novel is paramount. The author's biography or the history of his or her time is secondary at best. Readers find different readings, sometimes at the same time. These readings may undermine each other. The novel's meaning is, therefore, indeterminate and liquid. This concept taxes the reader's and the critic's imagination and intelligence. Deconstruction enriches reading by encouraging reader and critic to play with language, to continually reinterpret, and, ultimately, to leave things as they were for the next reader's encounter.

The Oath is a narrative quite conducive to a deconstructionist reading because Wiesel affirms the centrality of language in philosophy when he insists on the importance of both oral and written memory in the history of Judaism. Unlike Derrida, however, Wiesel privileges oral language, paradoxically, of course, because his main instrument of communication is the written word.

In *The Oath,* Wiesel contrasts oral and written language in Azriel, who uses his oral account of the destruction of his hometown to save the young man, while at the same time he holds and preserves the *Pinkas,* the written chronicle of Jewish Kolvillàg. Which is more significant? Arguably, Azriel's spoken words save a life. For Wiesel, the spoken word is therapeutic. He implies that a book is a supplement to oral experience and always requires some kind of mediation. But Wiesel is contradictory because, since he is not a TV or radio preacher, he must use the written word (as he does most effectively) to tell his stories, promote his political and historical views, and promulgate his much-needed moral perspective.

In *The Oath,* Wiesel is exerting pressure on the reader to recognize and admire the endurance of the Jewish people and to feel some degree of guilt for the Holocaust as well as for the long history of Jewish persecution before that event. Christians are expected to feel that their religion has failed humankind in its complicity with anti-Semitism or its inability to deflect the hatred of the uneducated masses. American Jews are indicted because they or their forebears seemingly did little to help their coreligionists and other endangered peoples during the twentieth century's long roll call of sectarian murders. These authorial intentions form the subtextual discourse at work in the narrative.

Ultimately, however, the meaning of *The Oath* derives from how the reader experiences the story. Many may agree with Alan Friedman's statement that *The Oath* is "a ghost of a work that has been willed into motion by a historical pain so genuine, so insistently close, that it can barely be forced to adopt the disguise of fiction" (A. Friedman 1973, 6).

10

Later Novels:
The Testament (1981),
The Fifth Son (1985),
The Forgotten (1992),
Twilight (1988), and
The Judges (2002)

The Testament, The Fifth Son, and *The Forgotten* represent a chronological and thematic change in what might be called Elie Wiesel's multivolume epic of the Holocaust. With the advent of the 1970s and in these novels, Wiesel turns his attention to "the birth and growth of the second generation of survivors" (D. Stern 1990, 63) as well as to the cold war and the plight of Jews in the Soviet Union. In *The Testament, The Fifth Son,* and *The Forgotten,* Wiesel continues his long journey from deep despair to dawning hope.

In *Twilight,* however, Wiesel resurrects the teenage male survivor character who figures in the early novels, places him as a grown-up in America, and makes him, like the author himself, a professor of literature and a scholar of mysticism no less. *Twilight* takes the Wiesel novel back into darkness—not the black night of the Holocaust, but a storm cloud in a mind going mad. Still, as Frederick Busch said in the *New York Times Book Review,* "Mr. Wiesel is our rememberer." For Busch, Wiesel is like a caretaker in the text who gathers up what history has denied or forgotten and preserves it for us through his own memory (Busch 1992, 8).

The Judges moves far away in events, place, and years from the Holocaust. Reminiscent of Jean-Paul Sartre's existential play *No Exit*, in which three mutually disliking acquaintances are condemned to spend eternity locked in a small, cheap, bare hotel room that symbolizes Hell, *The Judges* allegorically explores evil, guilt, selfishness, self-sacrifice, and love. Writing in the *New York Times*, Jonathan Rosen noted that in *The Judges*, Wiesel "is very good at creating an atmosphere in which ultimate questions have a natural place" (Rosen 2002, 41).

The Testament is a story concerning the oppression of Jewish writers in Stalin's Soviet Union. The background to the narrative is the fact that Stalin had many of the Soviet Union's greatest Jewish writers secretly executed in 1952. In *The Testament*, a man whose father was one of the murdered Jewish writers is given—after many years—the written testament of his father, Paltiel Kossover, who alone of the executed Jewish writers was permitted to leave behind a manuscript. Paltiel Kossover tells his life story: his Jewish boyhood in which he was beset by anti-Semitism in Czarist Russia, and when, after the Russian Revolution, he became a communist because of his hope for a better world; his moving to a small town in Romania with his Hasidic family; his life as a poet and journalist in the Paris of the 1920s; his idealist service in the Spanish Civil War when only the Soviet Union opposed German, Italian, and Spanish fascism; and his valiant service in the Soviet army in World War II as a stretcher-bearer and grave-digger.

Paltiel's return home is ill-fated: he made an unhappy marriage blessed only by the birth of his son; and toward the end of his life, he finally joined the Communist Party, which, ironically, soon falsely declared him a corrupt enemy and executed him.

In the course of studying the "testament" left for him by his father, the son, Grisha, comes to a better and useful understanding of his own life and his own times. With the scope of history embraced by Wiesel in *The Testament*, the author expands his writing horizon, but he remains committed to the discussion of the moral and ethical enigmas of the past century. *The Testament* is one of Wiesel's most skillfully written and engrossing novels.

Like *The Testament*, *The Fifth Son* is a story of the past framed by a son's perspective. In *The Fifth Son*, an unnamed son, the narrator, is alienated from his father because of the older man's reticence in talking about his Holocaust past. Frederic Morton, in the *New York Times Book Review,* stated that "In *The Fifth Son* the experience of surviving the Holocaust falls like a curtain between father and son. The book's action concerns the son's vain attempt to break through his father's unmerciful emotional veil" (Morton 1998, 8). The narrator learns of the death of a child-brother, Ariel, murdered in cold blood by the German commandant of a ghetto. The father had failed in a postwar assassination attempt on the former commandant, now a respected member of a German community, and the son sets out to complete a revenge that is against his basic values.

The title, *The Fifth Son,* is an oblique allusion to the Passover Haggadah (a text read at the Passover dinner) in which four sons are mentioned; a fifth son would have been a dead son. In the novel, the boy who was killed by the German commandant stands for the "missing" son. Writing in *The Christian Century,* Robert McAfee Brown reminds readers that *The Fifth Son,* like so many of Wiesel's works of fiction, deals in "probing questions" that refuse to let us settle comfortably into our faith and "lapse into indifference" (Brown 1985, 499). In this case, Wiesel deals with the question of the morality of revenge as well as the anguish people can feel when they suffer from a terrible event that they have not actually experienced (Shack 1986, 622).

The Forgotten tells the story of Elhanan Rosenbaum, a psychotherapist, a revered American university professor, a widower with a son in his forties, and a survivor who has an incurable disease, presumably Alzheimer's, that is causing him to lose his memory. Like many survivors of the Holocaust, Rosenbaum has never spoken of his experiences during World War II. Now, before his mind goes, he determines to inform his son, Malkiel, of his early life, and because of a crime that is haunting him, have his son visit the small Romanian town where he grew up. When the son hears what his father endured, he embarks on a quest to learn about the crime, and so he visits his father's birthplace. There the son learns the truth, and the truth is the cordage that paradoxically will bind the future generations together while liberating them.

Twilight reminds us that some Jewish families lost members in the Holocaust *and* in the Soviet gulags, Stalin's Siberian prisons. Stanley Moss, in the *New York Times Book Review,* emphasized the importance of family in *Twilight.* The novel shows us "how good the family is" as well as "how good people are" (Moss 1988, 12).

Raphael Lipkin, a professor of literature who studies mysticism, is the one member of his family to survive World War II and its aftermath.

Back in Poland in 1945 Lipkin, an orphaned survivor, age fifteen, was saved by a man named Pedro who worked for Briha, a Jewish rescue organization, and who may have lost his life in a gulag for having tried to save Raphael's brother Yoel, who has gone mad in a Russian prison hospital. Raphael has come temporarily to a psychiatric hospital in upstate New York ostensibly to work on the staff for a while and learn the relationship between madness and prophecy, but really to address his own problems: someone has been phoning him at midnight. He is haunted by the dead: he hears voices, and he talks to his dead parents. But most of all, he tells his suffering to the absent Pedro, his friend, his mentor, the man who brought him to Paris and then tried to save his brother but was caught and imprisoned by the Soviets. In losing Pedro, Raphael lost his father substitute. His guilt for surviving is a torment. (In *The Town beyond the Wall,* Pedro is also the mentor to the protagonist.) Raphael hopes against hope that Pedro escaped from Russia and is among the madmen in the clinic, as improbable as that is.

Lesley Chamberlain, in the *Times Literary Supplement,* has summarized Wiesel's tasks in *Twilight:* "how to relate to the dead and keep them from a new death, how to convey inconceivable loss, how to explain the memory of the extermination which, even the moment it happened, was impossible to grasp itself" (Chamberlain 1988, 1284).

Twilight is the time between day and night, between light and dark. Raphael is living in his "Twilight Zone." In the concentration camp, Raphael was in continual night. In America, where he has built a new, but not a happy, life, he is not yet and may never be fully in the light.

In *The Judges,* Wiesel moves into a literary subgenre: the psychological thriller, and the novel is far removed from the subject of the Holocaust. Although the story is related by a man who, like Michael in *The Town beyond the Wall,* was once a cold war prisoner tortured by communists in his native Romania, neither he nor any other of the main characters is a sole protagonist. Five passengers from an airliner forced down in a fierce New England snowstorm are held captive, as if they were hostages, by a sadistic, evil-worshipping man, who has set himself up as a judge of humankind. He is served by a hunchbacked servant who respects, fears, and hates him.

The "judge" forces the four men and one woman to reveal deep secrets in their lives and to prepare for the death of one of them, selected by themselves to be the least worthy of living, as a sacrifice to save the others. The captives experience frustration, anger, comradeship, and, most of all, terror as they explore their own lives, examine their consciences, and present evidence in mitigation and extenuation for why they and not one of the others should live that day.

Wiesel implies that judging is a dangerous, terrible, and maddening occupation. Wiesel as author is the ultimate judge of his creations. Or perhaps it is the reader who must judge? Regardless, the verdict is that all life is precious, and no one is more worthy to live than any other human being. Patrick Sullivan, in *Library Journal,* called *The Judges* "a triumphant affirmation of the power of love, honor, service and faith in human life" (Sullivan 2002, 198).

PLOT DEVELOPMENT

The Testament is the story of two generations of the men of a Russian Jewish family, the Kossovers, but especially Paltiel, the famous poet, and Grisha (*Grisha* is a Russian version of the biblical *Gershon*), his son. In typical Wiesel style, the two life stories entwine. In his testament, Paltiel recounts how he gave up on Judaism. He traveled to Berlin, Paris, Palestine, and Spain where he worked with communist groups and wrote poetry. As a journalist, he wrote articles hostile to Judaism that antagonized the Jewish press. Paltiel serves the Left in the Spanish Civil War from 1936 to 1939, and he serves the Allied cause in the Soviet army from 1941 to 1945. After World War II, he formally joined the Communist Party, but there and then he is subjected to vicious anti-Semitism that causes him to return to Judaism. Living once more in the town in which he was born, Paltiel takes up the Yiddish language again, and finds favor with the Jewish press that previously had attacked him. Finally, imprisoned and facing execution, he leaves a testament for his son so that Grisha will understand his father's life.

Grisha has a terrible life. He has no memory of his dead poet father. His mother has a lover whom Grisha hates. When the lover badgers Grisha about his father, the boy feels that the man is trying to usurp his father, and he bites his tongue in half, thus becoming a lifelong mute. When the male stenographer who had transcribed the testament, and who is an admirer of Paltiel's poetry, gives Grisha the testament, the boy has a parent's guidance for the rest of his life and for generations to come.

The plot of *The Fifth Son* is less credible than the plot of *The Testament* and of earlier Wiesel novels. The anticlimactic ending is a particular weakness in the narrative. The novel's strength lies in the suspense created as the German killers slowly strangle the Jewish community. In *The Fifth Son,* the unnamed narrator is trying to find out the secrets that his father, a Holocaust survivor, has kept from him. The silence of his father is a source of unhappiness for the son because that silence comes between the two men. The son wants his father's love, but his father seems to hold back. The son eventually learns that he had a brother, whom the German commandant of the ghetto tortured to death in front of his parents.

Furthermore, he learns that his father was a member of a group of Jews who, after the war, tried and failed to assassinate the murderous German SS official whom they called "The Angel of Death" and who destroyed the town in which the Jewish family lived. The father has been brooding over his part in the failed assassination, even thinking, wrongly, that an innocent person had been harmed. But the son finds out, through his father's friends and through old letters, that the Nazi official not only survived but is now a rich industrialist in Germany and respected by his community. The son then sets out obsessively to complete his father's revenge. When he finds and confronts the "Angel of Death," he cannot kill, and is satisfied leaving the German with his conscience. Revenge through conscience is the technique Wiesel had used earlier in *The Town beyond the Wall.*

In *The Forgotten,* Wiesel masterfully employs the double helix plot once more. The life stories of the father, Elhanan Rosenbaum, dying of Alzheimer's disease, and his son, Malkiel, a writer for the *New York Times,* unfold simultaneously. Elhanan's story is from memory, and Malkiel's is in the present—the 1980s. Elhanan grew up an Orthodox Jew in a Romanian town. Toward the end of World War II, Romania is occupied by Hungarian and German troops who, along with Romanian fascists, are determined to carry out the extermination of the Jewish population. Elhanan, a youth, is sent on a mission to Poland to see if it is true that the Germans are murdering the Jewish population there and will shortly begin the extermination of Hungarian and Romanian Jews. He finds that it is true, but is trapped in Poland where he saves himself from the death camps by joining a Jewish slave labor battalion sent to the Russian front to support the German army. There he escapes and joins a successful band of Jewish partisans fighting the Germans behind their lines. The advance of the Soviet army brings Elhanan to his hometown where he learns that his entire family has been deported to a death camp and killed.

As the Soviet army is liberating the town, the soldiers run amok, looting, and raping women. Elhanan's buddy, a Jew like Elhanan, begins, out of revenge, to rape a young woman whose husband was the worst of the fascists, torturing and killing Jews earlier in the war. Aghast at this injustice, Elhanan, tries to stop his friend but fails. That day and that failure lodge in Elhanan's mind for the rest of his life.

After the war is over, Elhanan meets a Palestinian Jewish woman. Together they fight their way to the Holy Land, then marry and begin a family. When the State of Israel declares independence in 1948, Elhanan joins the Haganah, the new Israeli army, and battles, unsuccessfully, to save the Old City of Jerusalem, where Jews have lived since the time of King David. Taken prisoner by the Arabs, Elhanan is released as the war ends, and returns home only to find that his wife died giving birth to their son.

Unable to live in the place where his beloved wife died, Elhanan emigrates to New York City, where kind relatives help him to build a new life for himself and a good life for his son, Malkiel, who is graduated from Columbia University in journalism and joins the *New York Times*. When Elhanan realizes that he is losing his memory, he slowly reveals his past and sends Malkiel off to Romania to see his father's grave and to confirm that his recollection of the day his soldier pal committed the outrage is correct.

Malkiel is trying to work out problems with the woman he loves in New York as he tries to locate a particular seventy-year-old woman who was raped in the town on liberation day in 1945, when many women were raped. With the help of a beautiful young Romanian interpreter—whose charms he resists—he manages the near impossible: the old woman is located. She confirms that his father had indeed tried to stop the rape, and that she was at least grateful for that because the attempt left her believing that not all men were evil.

Twilight's plot is complicated but brilliantly executed. The present story is that of Raphael Lipkin's descent into madness or near madness even as he is investigating the connection between madness and prophecy. We learn through flashbacks of his fortunate survival in the Holocaust, and his love for Pedro, his rescuer, who nevertheless fails to save Raphael's only surviving brother in the Soviet Union. Raphael's family life when he was a child, and the fate of his parents, three brothers, and two sisters receive full and graphic attention. These stories are painful to read because Wiesel has written of the Lipkin family's life and death with great tenderness and beauty. They are loving people.

In Lipkin's present life, we are informed that he is divorced and that he sorely misses his daughter Rachel. A clue to Lipkin's condition is the statement by his ex-wife to his young daughter that her father is mad.

The Judges is an engrossing thriller with a disappointing ending. In it, Wiesel has moved far from his iterative Holocaust subject. During a fierce blizzard and paralyzing snowstorm covering New England, a transatlantic passenger plane on its way to Tel Aviv, Israel, is forced to land on a deserted air strip in rural Connecticut. Passengers are rushed away to shelter by area residents; five are taken to a remote cabin by a man who calls himself the judge. There they are held prisoner and informed that one must die the next day. They are to be their own judges. We learn about the lives of the prisoners and wonder if they will be able to escape from their mad, sadistic captor and his hunch-backed servant. The captives, locked in their individual need to survive, never coalesce into a unit of action to overcome the judge, and are saved only because the hunchback has fallen in love with the female member of the group and, in hatred of his cruel master, stabs him to death.

In all of these late novels, Wiesel carefully constructs varying strands of suspense that keep the reader waiting until the end for closure to the main plots. And Wiesel, the skilled storyteller, generally provides satisfactory closure.

SETTINGS

Wiesel has not been reluctant to experiment as a novelist. Just as the boy surviving the Holocaust plot is the signature Wiesel plot in his early novels, the ambiguous and sometimes fragmented narrative is a Wiesel signature in his middle narratives (Davis 1994, 62). The image of a double helix comes to mind as one reads the entwining narratives of father and son in *The Testament.* The geographical backgrounds of *The Testament* are varied: Russia, Romania, France, Spain, and Israel. *The Fifth Son* takes us to a shtetl in the Carpathian Mountains, Brooklyn, Manhattan, and Germany. *The Forgotten* inhabits a Romanian town in the Carpathians, Poland, Russia, Israel, and New York City.

Wiesel's descriptive abilities grow as his writing career continues. The descriptions of Paltiel's service in the Soviet army and Elhanan's service with the partisans in World War II are unsurpassed in any of the author's novels after *Night.* Also provocative and outstanding is Wiesel's description of the battle for Jerusalem in 1948.

The setting of *Twilight* is the Mountain Clinic, a psychiatric hospital for the insane. Raphael Lipkin goes to the mountain warehouse of the insane because he thinks he is losing his mind, and because there he will find the mad prophets who are the only people capable of making sense of the mad world. The place is a microcosm of the world of Holocaust survivors and, indeed, the contemporary world itself—for all people alive today, even if we were not actually born before or during the Holocaust, are survivors in a sense. The Holocaust happened. It was the salient event of the twentieth century. It did more to undermine belief in God than anything since the Black Death in the fourteenth century. Yes, we are alive, but we are different because our world seems without even the illusion of an orderly universe, a progressive humankind, and, most of all, a God taking notice. Paul Taylor, in the London *Times,* stated that Wiesel's "principal speculation [is] about the possible insanity in the nature of the universe" (Taylor 1988, G6).

The Judges has only one setting: a room in a log cabin in the Connecticut woods. The windows are sealed and unbreakable. The door is electronically controlled from the outside. The setting is like the set of a domestic drama, and the few characters, seven, also remind the reader of a play scene.

CHARACTER DEVELOPMENT

There are two main and fully developed characters in *The Testament:* Paltiel and Grisha. Paltiel, a poet, is the only Wiesel protagonist who is a creative writer. Paltiel's book of poetry is called *I Saw My Father in a Dream* (269), but none of the poems in the collection refer to his father, a Hasidic businessperson and the son of a distinguished Hasidic rabbi. He needs the approval of his father, as most people do, and when he receives a letter from his father in which the older man informs his son that he has read disturbing political comments by an author with the same name as his son, Paltiel is hurt. His father and all the rest of his family are killed when the Holocaust engulfs Romania. They are buried in a trench with hundreds of other murdered Jews. When Paltiel stands before the filled-in trench as the Red army liberates the Romanian town in which his family had lived, he commences his return to Judaism, an event his father fervently had wished for. Paltiel's father's spirit comes back to guide the poet son.

Grisha is a mostly silent character, obviously because he destroyed his tongue as a child, but also because he grew up in the Soviet Union, a society where in order to survive—especially if you were Jewish—silence was safety. Grisha does not develop much, but he serves as a vehicle for the telling of a historically powerful tale of misplaced altruism, betrayal, suffering, and unhappiness: his father's story—the Russian Jew's story in the twentieth century.

As in *The Testament,* there are two fully developed characters in *The Fifth Son:* Reuven Tamiroff and his unnamed son, the story's narrator. As in *The Testament,* the two main characters are father and son. The father in *The Fifth Son,* Reuven Tamiroff, like Paltiel in *The Testament,* rebels against his Jewish upbringing, but not quite to the extent that Paltiel does. Reuven found his Judaism a handicap to his academic career, which turned out to be brilliant. When the German army invades, he becomes the Jewish community's leader during the persecutions. His actions are heroic. Yet he is cold and distant to his son because he is distracted and depressed by the memory of his Holocaust past, the terrible fate of his community, the murder of his older child, and his failure to revenge the community. He will never recover joy in life despite his affection for Hasidism.

The unnamed son (sometimes he calls himself by his dead brother's name—Ariel) is an American youth, a college student in the rebellious 1960s, a period Wiesel denigrates in the text. This character, like almost all of Wiesel's young male protagonists, desperately wants the love of his father. His attempt at revenging the injuries the "Angel of Death" has done to his family is his homage to his father's courage and an attempt to assuage his father's long-term misery.

A lesser character is Richard Lander, the ruthless, cunning, sadistic German commander of the Davarowsk ghetto in the Carpathian Mountains, a place of hell he has established and over which he rules in order to destroy the Jewish inhabitants. His sobriquet, the Angel of Death, is appropriate. He is a histrionic person, reveling in the performance of power and exceedingly cruel. The character is somewhat overdone, however, nearly resulting in the depiction of a villainous Nazi caricature.

Elhanan Rosenbaum, in *The Forgotten,* is a particularly well-constructed character. We experience almost his entire life, an epic journey in Eastern European and Middle Eastern history. His slow descent into the oblivion of Alzheimer's disease is accompanied by unfolding revelations of his trauma-filled life that engage his son, Malkiel, and bind the latter into the family history. Malkiel's character is not as well developed, but then he is the medium through which his father's memory works. Elhanan has inscribed his testament on Malkiel's mind as the last act of a Jewish father intent on inculcating his son with the profound ethics of the Jewish faith, ethics that are not mere words, but that require, and even demand, righteous action.

The main character in *Twilight,* really the only fully developed one, is Raphael Lipkin, and he thinks he is going mad. He questions the reason for his survival. It seems so random and so pointless that his faith in God is shaken. He came to the psychiatric hospital to work on the question of the relationship between madness and prophecy. But he also came because the man who was calling him at midnight disparaged his friend Pedro, while hinting that Pedro was alive and at the Mountain Clinic. The voice persuades Lipkin to go there. Just as Lipkin was about to go home at the end of his stay, he finds himself in a nighttime conversation with one of the patients. The patient believes he is God. In the conversation, Lipkin first comes to think that the man is the midnight caller. Then, as they continue to talk, Lipkin is convinced that he is actually talking to God. He castigates God for what he has allowed to happen to the human race, and God is penitent. Raphael Lipkin may be mad after all, and may never in fact leave the Mountain Clinic. The encounter between Lipkin and "God" is one of Wiesel's most brilliant passages in all his novels.

The few characters in *The Judges* are among the best developed in all of Wiesel's fiction. The judge is all-powerful in his domain. There, he is like God (117). But, with his devotion to evil and death, he really is more like Satan (181–87). His servant, the hunchback, was saved by the judge after he was seriously injured and badly burned in a car accident that killed his parents, and although he has been loyal to the judge for years, he has grown to hate the cruel fiend.

Razziel Friedman, a fifty-year-old widower, who is an ordained Orthodox rabbi and director of a yeshiva, has the intellectual ability and experience to counter the clever arguments of the judge. Razziel, who was tortured by communists in his homeland, Romania, and who lost his memory of his childhood and family as a result, was on the way to Israel to find the man who could tell him about his family. Despite his experiences in Romania, Razziel finds it difficult to believe that someone would want to kill several innocent people who in a random way have come into his life.

Bruce Schwarz is an aging Don Juan who has seduced and hurt many women. He thought that love was a game, like a tennis match, to win and then go on to take on other players. He is dressed somewhat flamboyantly, as if he were still a roué. But now he was going to Israel to locate a former girlfriend to try to make amends for treating her cruelly. Belatedly, he realizes that he truly loves her and wants to make his life with her. Oversure of himself, he is at first unwilling to take the Judge seriously. He wants to live in order to redeem himself.

Claudia is a beautiful young divorcée who works in the theater. She has been disappointed in love, but now she is full of hope because she has just started a new love affair with a man whom she met in New York City and who is living in Israel. She was on her way to join him. Claudia cannot conceive that her life, now full of joy, could possibly end because of a whim of a seeming madman.

Yoav is an Israeli commando who was in the States for treatment for an inoperable and soon-to-be fatal brain tumor. He was on his way home to spend his last few months with his wife, whom he loves deeply. He has been thinking about the meaning of his life as it seems to be coming to an end. Being a man of action, he immediately thinks of means to escape but does not know it can be achieved as a group. Anyway, his personal sorrow holds him back.

George Kirsten is an unhappily married man, with a mistress he cares for more than his cold and angry wife. He has discovered a Holocaust secret that will bring a war criminal to justice and was on his way to Israel to inform Israeli authorities. His pursuit of justice has become the center of his life, and it has given his life real meaning for once.

All of the strangers from the plane are interesting and distinct people. We share in their ruminations on their past and how their actions have brought them to this moment and this place. They have their stories to tell, and through these stories, the reader comes to care for them all, hoping, seemingly against hope, that they will survive and carry out the missions that caused them to take a fateful flight to Tel Aviv in the winter. They do.

THEMATIC ISSUES

From *Night* on, a recurring theme in Wiesel's novels is the loss of the father or the emotional separation of a son from his father. In *The Testament*, the son is trying to learn about the life and times of his long-dead father. In *The Fifth Son*, the son tries to find the reason for his father's emotional distance, and when he learns the reason, like Hamlet, he embarks on a journey of revenge. Surely, the sad father fixation evidenced in Wiesel's fiction is the result of the traumatic loss of his father in the concentration camp in which the author was last held (Davis 1994, 141–45). The Wiesel son often suffers from guilt at the loss of the father. Significantly, in *The Testament,* as his son is about to be circumcised in the traditional Jewish ritual, Paltiel gives the infant his own father's name. It is both an act of continuity and a way of alleviating guilt. Perhaps all of Wiesel's fiction stands as an act of mourning for the good father he could not save from the murdering Nazis?

In both *The Testament* and *The Fifth Son,* father and son no longer battle. There is no need to attack paternal authority. The father becomes the object of love—and it is a true and fulfilling love. The binding factor in the father-son dynamic is the overriding condition of Jewishness. Paltiel's main message to Grisha is that his great guilt is that he did not live like his Hasidic father. "I lived a communist and I die a Jew" (21). He admonishes Grisha that a Jew should live with his brothers, and thus Grisha makes his way to Israel. Wiesel once more signifies the continuity of Judaism from father to son and, to extrapolate, from mother to daughter, or, better, from generation to generation.

In *The Fifth Son,* the new Wiesel theme comes into focus: the pain of the children of survivors, people who did not experience the Holocaust and as a result have found an almost unbridgeable void between them and their parents. They feel an inexplicable shame that their parents could have let terrible things happen to them, as if the parents had control of their fate. And the children of survivors have a void in their lives because they did not experience Hitler's war against the Jews and thus were not witness to the greatest historical catastrophe in the saga of the Jewish people since the destruction of Jerusalem in 70 A.D. (192).

Because of his great personal compassion, Wiesel introduces the theme of compassion for young Germans, who are innocent of their parents' evil deeds. As a rational human being, Wiesel opposes—as all should—the concept of collective guilt (196).

In *The Forgotten,* Wiesel returns to the theme of the importance of remembering. Young Jewish people now and in the future must know the story of their ancestors, who underwent the greatest trauma of the twentieth century. In not forgetting, they will maintain the continuity of the Jewish people. In not forgetting, they may be armed to prevent a holocaust from happening to Jews again, or, indeed, to any beleaguered ethnic or racial minority.

In *The Forgotten,* as the generation of Holocaust survivors is dying off, the father-son relationship, again central to a Wiesel narrative, revolves around the concept of stewardship. The children must be informed. Regardless of the pain and emotional cost of recollection, the shame of misdeeds or cowardice, the loss of faith, the fearsome dreams in the night, or action-freezing depression, the generations to come must know the story of the truly lost generation of European Jews. Their memory must survive too. The father-son theme in Wiesel's fiction often ends with the death of the father, coming after reconciliation and understanding. In a way, Wiesel's sons become their fathers upon the death of the elders.

Wiesel's main theme in *Twilight* is his boldest: Humans have a right to be disappointed in God, to confront the Deity, to ask God where he was when all the children were being killed in the camps, and to indict God for neglect of the human race he created. It is as if Wiesel, like Lipkin, has gone mad from mourning, and is raging against the spirit he sardonically calls "Merciful God, God of Love" (208).

In *The Judges,* Wiesel's main theme is the morality of judgment. Although all of us judge our fellow human beings much of the time, who really has the wisdom and the right to judge? Surely not self-appointed judges, bereft of mercy, who through force have taken power over the lives of others. Although *The Judges* was first published in France in 1999, the novel seems particularly current and applicable to world conditions in the first years of the twenty-first century, when Wiesel says that "only fanatics—in religion as well as politics—can find a meaning in someone else's death" (188).

The Judges is also thematically concerned with the relationship between good and evil. Wiesel's perspective here is Manichaean, a belief that the forces of good and evil exist simultaneously and struggle eternally in the world. The judge is a satanic figure embodying the very evil he worships. Razziel the rabbi takes the side of good in his life-and-death debate with the judge (181–87). In the end, Razziel wins, but only because the hunchback decides he can no longer serve evil. As so often in history, the temporary victory of good over evil is a near thing.

ALTERNATE READING: A MARXIST CRITICAL READING

Based on the writings of the nineteenth-century German philosopher Karl Marx (1818–1883), Marxism in its most extreme form—

Communism—has been thoroughly discredited as a political system. Marxism also collapsed as an economic system because its insistence on central economic planning eliminated institutions that could ensure that manpower and resources were used prudently. But Marx himself had a messianic socialistic dream of equality and justice for all, which stemmed from the moral vision of the prophets of the Hebrew Bible and the humanistic values of the French Revolution and of Romanticism. He appealed to what he thought was the better nature of humankind, exhorting people to give to society all that they were capable of giving and to take from society only what they needed. Marx saw labor as the source of the true value in goods and services. He believed that social life responded almost entirely to economic needs. Everything human beings do relates basically to their need for food, shelter, work, clothing, goods, and money to pay for other necessities of life.

Perhaps Marx's most controversial argument, gleaned from Georg Wilhelm Friedrich Hegel, a late eighteenth-, early nineteenth-century German philosopher, is that growth comes only through the struggle of opposites. Thus class conflict is inevitable because capitalists will not fairly share the wealth that comes from inheritance and ownership with the workers who produce that wealth. Marx had one of the great intellects of the nineteenth century. His ethical passion and explanatory skill echo in the halls of government and academe even today.

Just as Freud tried to explain the psychological roots of literature, Marx, decades earlier, attempted to show the economic and social roots of literature. He located the production of literary work in the economic and political fabric of the time in which the work is or was produced. A novel is a commodity that reflects the values of the dominant class in the society for which it is meant. Writers either overtly or intuitively know this, and they also know that they must accommodate power or lose the opportunity to be published and read.

In the past, Marxist literary criticism highlighted historical readings and placed the text within its historical context as it interacted with the politics and the power of its time. Contemporary Marxist criticism concentrates on the ideological significance of a work. It holds that because the dissemination of the literary work is controlled by those in power, then the ideological values of the dominant class of the time are generally to be found in most works of literature—or the literary work may be subversive, secretly or openly attempting to undermine the values of those who have the power. Today's Marxist critics locate and expose the significant social and political truths in the literary work, most importantly its ideological mission: endorsement or subversion.

The Testament attacks the Fascism and anti-Semitism that engulfed much of Europe in the 1930s and 1940s. It points out how thinking Jewish socialists had hoped that the desire of Marx for a more equitable world society would prevail. But Marxism was diverted and perverted by Communism's corruption and antihumanism everywhere, even in Spain during the Spanish Civil War. Wiesel can be called a Jewish socialist. He is sympathetic toward the plight of the poor and the suffering everywhere in the world. He would certainly embrace the Marxist credo: "From each according to his/her ability. To each according to his/her needs."

But a Marxist literary critic, following the dictum that the individual is less important than the common good, would dislike the individuality of *The Testament,* that the narrative does not generalize about the human condition but specifies the Jewish experience. Some would fault *The Testament's* "shattering of . . . communist dreams and hopes," as did Robert McAfee Brown in *Christian Century* (1981, 651). Others would fault Wiesel for commodifying the Holocaust, making it his business, so to speak. That feeling of commodification grows stronger when in *Twilight,* Wiesel seems to reiterate his basic Holocaust narrative, the experience of remembering a boyhood in the cataclysmic event. The only difference in *Twilight* is that the protagonist is from Poland, not Romania.

The Judges can be faulted because the five prisoners of the judge cannot act collectively. They do not stand as a group against the tyranny, and each plays the judge's game in thinking of ways to justify his or her individual right to survive before the others in their desperate community.

When once more Wiesel valorizes Israel, in *The Testament, The Fifth Son,* and *The Judges,* a nation that emerged in the explosion of nationalism in the twentieth century, he is faulted by Marxist critics who, as socialists, are naturally internationalists. Contemporary Marxist critics would see the centrality of Judaism to the narrative of *The Testament* and *The Fifth Son,* as well as most other Wiesel texts, as a retrogressive force, narrowly and oppressively ideological. On the other hand, Wiesel's insistence on the importance of righteous political action, even an individual act such as the son's attempt to revenge his father in *The Fifth* Son, is most acceptable to Marxist critics. And some Marxists critics would see Wiesel's active support of Israel in his fiction as a valid and understandable use of literature for ideological purposes.

Most of all, Wiesel's religiosity—sometimes mystical—violates the Marxist philosophy of dialectical materialism: the argument that economics and material needs dominate the human story, and that the universal phenomenon of racism is based to a large extent on class conflict. Stated simply, the rise of totalitarianism in the twentieth century was brought about by the conflict between capitalists and workers through the exploitation of the latter by the former.

In *The Testament, The Fifth Son, The Forgotten,* and *Twilight,* all the main characters are middle class, privileged in varying degrees, educated people more committed to their personal development and gain than to the collective good, and even when circumstances force them to live, work, and die together, they remain apart from the proletariat. Their common cause, so to speak, is uncommon. When there is a commitment beyond self, it is for the survival of a religion or for the survival of the State of Israel, a nation that developed from one of many nationalist movements in the nineteenth century and, with the impetus of the reformulation of defunct empires, with the Treaty of Versailles in 1919. A commitment to a nationalist movement is antithetical to Socialism, which is international in scope.

The Judges differs from the other four novels in this chapter in that class is insignificant in the text. As a thriller, the novel does not concentrate on economic matters, either. The emphases are on theodicy, morality, and religion. With the exception of morality, these topics are of less interest to Marxist critics.

Wiesel's ideology stems in part from a degree of Puritanism that reflects his sincere religious—Hasidic—background. His insistence that one can make sense of the world—despite the seeming mindless, chaotic nature of contemporary life—only through a dialogue with God, is antithetical to the Marxist view that economic determinism is the only valid way—the "scientific" way—of understanding humankind's history and its future. A Marxist critical reading of the novels would indict rabbinical control and passivity as serving the dominant fascist culture in Europe from 1939 to 1945 in that rabbinical leadership too often focused more on finding salvation through prayers for God's intervention than on violently resisting the growing fascist tyranny.

Besides being a humanitarian, a philosopher, and a creative writer, Elie Wiesel is a religious person. He is an Orthodox Jew with a deep affection for, and appreciation of, Hasidism. Marx opposed religion. He saw preaching of any kind as an act of capitalist commerce. At worst, religion was used by the dominant class to keep the masses down. Furthermore, when religious leaders such as rabbis, priests, ministers, or imams preach tribal exclusivity, they may be fostering ideological aspects of racism, which may be used to rationalize exploitation, and which, in the long run, can place nations or peoples on a moving walkway that leads from social discrimination to genocide.

Last, Marxist critics would join with feminist critics to fault the male-centered aspects of Wiesel's later novels. The protagonists are always men, and women are passive for the most part. Men act, hide, fight, and sometimes escape. Conversely, women wait and die, except when they are sexually aggressive toward the reluctant protagonist. That may be as it was, but the stereotypes are unrelenting, as, for example, the cloying cliché of the saintly, self-sacrificing, Jewish mother and grandmother.

11

Selected Nonfiction

AUTOBIOGRAPHY

Elie Wiesel has written two autobiographies. *All Rivers Run to the Sea*, published in 1995, presents the author's life from childhood until 1969. *And the Sea Is Never Full*, published in 1999, depicts Wiesel's life from 1969 to 1995. Both memoirs take their titles from the same passage in Ecclesiastes from which Ernest Hemingway found his title for his first novel, *The Sun Also Rises*.

What profit hath a man of all his labor which he taketh under the sun? One generation passeth away, and another generation cometh; but the earth abideth forever. The sun also riseth, and the sun goeth down, and hasteth to his place where he arose. . . . All rivers run to the sea; yet the sea is not full; unto the place from whence the rivers come, thither they return again. All things are full of labor; man cannot utter it: the eye is not satisfied with seeing, nor the ear filled with hearing.

All Rivers Run to the Sea begins with Wiesel's dream of his father (Shlomo Wiesel), whom he lost in a German concentration camp in 1945. Wiesel says that he never really knew his father, but that he loved his parent deeply. This is a fact obvious to readers of Wiesel's fiction, in which, again and again, the father figure is treated with love, respect, and even reverence. The father of Wiesel's memory, both in fiction and in memoir, is manly but gentle, religious but not fanatic, devoted to serving his fellow Jews but not at the expense of his family, and seldom given to exercise parental authority. But in the memoir, the father is portrayed a little more realistically, such as when Wiesel notes that as a child, he sometimes was afraid of his father (5).

But Wiesel did have a happy Carpathian Mountain childhood in the small Romanian town of Sighet. His account of that idyllic childhood makes for a substantial opening portion of *All Rivers Run to the Sea.* But the second half of the "Childhood" section is appropriately called "Darkness," and it too begins with Wiesel dreaming about his father. The events of "Darkness" are well known to Wiesel readers. That section of Childhood—it covers only some sixteen months—is also the end of childhood for Wiesel. His maturity came fast and hard in the concentration camps, and his survival against great odds evidenced his inner strength, the power of youth, and the young man's determination to live. Faith was lost in the process, and regained later. Interestingly, the "Childhood" section also ends with Wiesel addressing the memory of his father, who has no real grave and is only "a fistful of ashes" (99).

Elie Wiesel, the man on his own, no longer dreams of Shlomo Wiesel. At the end of the memoir, however, Wiesel, age forty, dreams of his mother, Sarah Feig Wiesel, with whom he had even less time than he had with his father. She was gassed to death and her body cremated in the ovens of Auschwitz shortly after she arrived in the death camp in March 1944.

Subsequent sections of *All Rivers Run to the Sea* are not subdivided. Wiesel proceeds to "Schooling" in France and the ten-year period when he could not talk, let alone write, about his concentration camp experience; his early writing in "Journalist," along with his happiness at the founding of the State of Israel, the refuge for surviving Jews; "Travelling" to India, Canada, and elsewhere; living in "Paris," where and when he met François Mauriac, who inspired him to write *Night;* friends and political events in "New York"; the early reception of his work in "Writing" as well as the revelation of how he met a beautiful and sophisticated "young mother of Austrian descent in the process of getting a divorce" (338) and who became Mrs. Wiesel in "Jerusalem," the last section of the memoir and the one in which Wiesel discusses one of the most important historical events in his life—the Six-Day War in which his beloved Israel survives the concentrated attack of the Arab world.

All Rivers Run to the Sea ends with Wiesel still questioning the meaning of life and the intentions of God, but wishing that he could say to his long-deceased father: "Don't worry, your son will try to be a good Jew" (418).

And the Sea Is Never Full continues Wiesel's life story from 1969 to July 1995, when he made another return to Sighet. There he visits the Jewish cemetery and thinks of all those murdered Jews who have no graves, and then takes a train to Auschwitz and Buchenwald, reliving the great trauma of his adolescence. He thinks of his father again and wishes that Shlomo Wiesel could advise him about the rest of his life (409).

In *And the Sea Is Never Full,* Wiesel is a world-class celebrity and the conscience of humankind. One of the most fascinating revelations in the memoir is the way Wiesel respectfully but firmly admonishes world leaders such as President Ronald Reagan and President Lech Walesa of Poland. Wiesel castigates them for insensitivity to the memory of Jewish survivors of the Holocaust. In the section "François Mitterrand and Jewish Memory," Wiesel, upon discovering that a long-term friend, President François Mitterrand of France, hid his collaboration with the Germans in World War II and was unrepentant about his part in the fascist Vichy government of France under German occupation, breaks off the long and deep friendship.

In "Crossroads," he is about to be married when Teddy Kollek, the mayor of Jerusalem, calls him for advice. Wiesel is a friend of Golda Meir, the first woman prime minister of Israel. He discusses military strategy with the commander-in-chief of the Israeli army. But the personal is ever present in his memoirs, for in this period of great political activity, his son, Elisha, is born. Wiesel has at last overcome the fear of bringing new life into a world that could spawn an Auschwitz.

In "Scars," Wiesel, who never completed an academic degree, is appointed Distinguished Professor of Jewish Studies in the City College (now City University) of New York. Then the Yom Kippur War, in which Egypt and Syria attacked Israel on the holiest and most solemn day of the Jewish calendar, finds Wiesel despondent because the Jewish nation must fight desperately for its life again while most of the world, except for the United States, looks on with indifference. Fortunately, Israeli arms finally triumph after terrible losses. In the aftermath of the war, Wiesel meets and comes to admire the brilliant United States Secretary of State Henry Kissinger, himself a Jewish refugee from Nazi Germany. It is Wiesel, perhaps among others, who strongly suggests that the Israeli government invite President Anwar Sadat to Jerusalem, an act that led to peace between Israel and Egypt after almost thirty years of hostilities.

In "On Human Rights," Wiesel attacks the genocidal atrocities of the Khmer Rouge in Cambodia, and supports the Armenian attempt to get Turkey to acknowledge the mass murder of Armenians in World War I. In 1987, Wiesel and his wife go to Hiroshima to meet survivors of the first use of a nuclear weapon. He is haunted by the walls bearing shadows of incinerated people.

"On Learning and Teaching" shows Wiesel doing battle for human rights for Arab prisoners in Israel, and admonishing Israeli politicians who believe that one can be a good Jew only if one lives in Israel. Wiesel knows that good Jews live and serve God and Israel in the Diaspora while some Jewish scoundrels live in the Jewish state.

In "Reviews and Polemics," Wiesel laments that his once good relationship with Simon Wiesenthal, the renowned Nazi hunter, soured over the latter's disappointment and resentment that Wiesel and not he was awarded the Nobel Peace Prize (127–31).

"On Becoming a Speaker" shows Wiesel on the lecture circuits. He shares experiences, some humorous, others confrontational, as anti-Semites and Holocaust deniers insult or attack him. The seemingly insane people Wiesel has met in his lifetime are the subjects of "Of Madmen and Visionaries." Filmmakers try to make movies faithful to Wiesel's novels, but their films for Wiesel's medium "remains the word, not the image" (164).

"Cardinal Lustiger, My Friend" informs the reader of how Wiesel met and became friends with Jean-Marie Lustiger, a converted Polish Jew whose mother was killed at Auschwitz, and whom Pope John Paul II appointed Archbishop of Paris. Lustiger insists that he is still a Jew even though he converted to Catholicism, whereas Wiesel believes that no one can embrace two religions. Nevertheless, the two men become friends, and Lustiger supports Jewish causes. "A Museum in Washington" and "Words of Remembrance" deal with Wiesel's part in the creation of the Holocaust Museum in Washington, D.C., a task President Jimmy Carter asked him to undertake when Wiesel was appointed to the President's Commission on the Holocaust Memorial. In preparation for the task, Wiesel goes to Poland to see Auschwitz for the first time since he left it in early 1945. It is an incredibly painful experience for him. The museum project finally comes to fruition under President Bill Clinton.

In "The Bitburg Affair," Wiesel fails to keep President Reagan from falling into a trap laid by Prime Minister Helmut Kohl of the German Federal Republic to get the president to whitewash Nazi SS and other

German troops of World War II, who were guilty of perpetrating or supporting horrible atrocities against Jews, Poles, Russians, and even American soldiers, by visiting a cemetery for German war dead and making a speech in which he states that these Germans were also "victims" (241).

The climax of *And the Sea Is Never Full* is in the section entitled "From Sighet to Oslo," in which Wiesel receives the Nobel Peace Prize. In "Encounters," the Nobel laureate travels the world on missions for human rights, and in the brief "Chronicle of a Deposition," Wiesel recounts his appearance at the trial of a French citizen who collaborated with the Germans in World War II and who helped organize the torture, deportation, and murder of Jews. "The Gulf War" and "The Destiny of Sarajevo" concern the conflicts of the 1990s as American and NATO powers strive to contain brutal dictatorships and new genocides.

In "Three Suicides," Wiesel meditates on the suicide of famous Holocaust survivors, trying to understand their frustrations, weaknesses, and feelings of guilt. Wiesel explores, in "Understand," why he chooses to undergo the rigors and pain of writing fiction when he could do other, easier things with his life. His answer to himself is that writing helps him to understand himself. Wiesel discusses the mission of the Wiesel Foundation for Humanity in "The Anatomy of Hate" as he marshals Nobel Peace Prize winners to support him in his war on hatred.

Finally, in "As Yet," Wiesel explains how the memory of his father, and his dreams of Shlomo Wiesel, help him to overcome the pain he experiences in writing the literary "fictions" he needs to produce. He also must deal with his guilt feelings that in writing about subjects other than the Holocaust—the bulk of his writing, especially nonfiction—he is failing the dead. A return in 1995 to Sighet leaves him wondering if he should let others tell the sad story of the end of five hundred years of Jewish life in Central and Eastern Europe. But he is told by many to "wager on the future" (410). He wants his father to help him. Is Shlomo calling his son Elie to join him in death? Wiesel leaves us and himself with the question (411).

Although *And the Sea Is Never Full* is not quite as personal as *All Rivers Run to the Sea*, it is the perfect complement to the early work. It provides a history lesson, and a primer of humanitarianism, as Elie Wiesel, the chronicler of the Holocaust, becomes a spokesperson for justice and compassion in a world already forgetting the painful lessons of World War II. Wiesel's two biographies remind readers how skillful a prose writer he is. His honesty, sincerity, and commitment to human dignity shine like a directional beacon in a dark world filled with cruelty and irrational hatred.

ESSAYS

Legends of Our Time was written twenty years after Elie Wiesel was liberated from Buchenwald concentration camp. During those years, he traveled through much of the world and met many fascinating people. In *Legends of Our Time,* Wiesel first writes about the death of his father. Then he honors his early teachers who taught him to respect language and to love the past. He meets a concentration camp overseer in Israel and confronts him with his evil actions. Wiesel goes on to portray his life in Paris where he meets a homeless man who speaks thirty languages and who believes he knows all the secrets of the universe. Then there is the time he was asked by a young worker in Spain to translate an ancient Spanish Jewish document because the man thinks his ancestors may be Jewish.

Wiesel's early life (indeed his whole life) was filled with fascinating incidents, and the storyteller enjoys recalling them as well as discussing the people who had a great influence on his life. He cautions the reader, however, to be careful about language: it can mend anything. It can even attain the quality of deeds. Wiesel seems to be hinting that memory is frail, and that any writer may at any given time be self-serving in his or her narration.

One Generation After is a long meditation brought on by the fact that twenty-five years after Wiesel was transported to Auschwitz, he returned to Sighet. Ostensibly, he has come to retrieve the Bar Mitzvah watch he buried when the German, Hungarian, and Romanian fascists were about to deport him, his parents and his three sisters. Wiesel finds the watch, but decides to leave it where he hid it because there are no Jews left in the little town, and the watch will serve as a monument to what Sighet has lost. Perhaps someone, generations from now, will find the watch and it will cause them to reflect that once a Jewish community thrived in Sighet. It is as important for him to create a memorial as it is for him to write about the Holocaust, because one cannot truly write "the ineffable" (Berenbaum 1979, 94, 142). To be a witness to a terrible event is to live in frustration, waiting for the world to change, but of course it won't.

Wiesel remembers friends and events in his childhood. He thinks about Adolf Eichmann, the German impresario of death, who helped plan the Holocaust and was its chief administrator. Wiesel is puzzled that such an ordinary man could have been responsible for the death of so many millions of people while never thinking of his actions as anything more than a job well done. Wiesel worries that people have forgotten the lessons of the Holocaust. He considers the state of the world as he is writing, and he finds it deplorable. Human rights are being violated everywhere (then and now). Wiesel also takes on young Germans who forgot what their fathers did, and who now are anti-Semites in their Leftward leaning. Twenty-five years after the Holocaust, Wiesel was not a happy person. The world had let him down. It had started to forget.

A Jew Today not only talks about being Jewish, but also discusses the Biafra rebellion in Nigeria during which the world looked on passively when so many people starved to death. Wiesel states his unhappiness with Aleksandr Solzhenitsyn because the Nobel Prize–winning refugee author loves Czarism and is indifferent to the fate of Jews under Stalin's reign of terror. Wiesel's feelings about South Africa and apartheid are clear: he is totally against racism in any form, and he is glad that South African Jews have supported the liberal, antiracist elements in South African society regardless of the cost to themselves in terms of security.

Wiesel also offers a poignant sketch of his maternal grandfather, the Hasid Dodye Feig, whom he dearly loved. Finally, he states the duties and responsibilities of "A Jew Today": he must fight despair. He must keep the spirit of the Sabbath. Jews must remember that Jewish strength is not "geography" but history (160). And Jews must always celebrate life.

From the Kingdom of Memory: Reminiscences contains Wiesel's Nobel address in which he accepted the Peace Prize on December 10, 1986, in Oslo, Norway, and the Nobel lecture that he gave the next day. In the former, Wiesel makes it clear that he has no right to speak for all the Jewish victims of the Holocaust, nor does he deserve to be honored on their behalf (232). He spoke as a Jew concerned with anti-Semitism in the world, the way Soviet Jewry was being treated, and how Jews in Arab lands were suffering. He spoke out for Nelson Mandela and other political victims of racism and oppression. And he called for peace between both parties in the Holy Land (234).

Not surprisingly, Wiesel's Nobel lecture begins by affirming his belief in the coming of the Messiah. And then, also not surprisingly, he offers a legend of the Baal Shem Tov. Wiesel goes on to explain that he has tried to understand how the highly cultured German people could commit such atrocities in the Holocaust, or why good and great men such as Franklin Delano Roosevelt and Winston Churchill could have been so indifferent to what was happening to the Jewish citizens of Germany, Poland, and Russia (241). Also, Wiesel calls upon the people of the world not to forget the Holocaust, and not to abandon Israel, the ancestral home of the Jewish people and the refuge of Jewish survivors then, now, and in the future.

Also in *From the Kingdom of Memory,* Wiesel states that he writes so as not to forget. His novels always include the people he is most fascinated with: Hasidim, children, old men, beggars. Words themselves are artifacts and sacred for Wiesel, a belief derived from Hasidism. In a moving personal essay, Wiesel celebrates friendship. But his best friend, the one more than any other he could unburden his heart to, is long dead. It was his father.

HASIDIC TALES AND BIBLE STUDIES

HASIDIC TALES

Elie Wiesel's maternal grandfather was a devout Hasid. As a boy, Elie was more drawn to Hasidism than to his father's rationalism and traditional Orthodox Judaism. For many years, Wiesel and his family have resided in New York City near the Hasidic communities in Brooklyn. He admires, perhaps even envies, the joy, loyalty, structure, and conviction of Hasidism. It is not surprising that the storyteller loves Hasidic legends and often includes them in his fiction.

The Hasidic tale is not studied like the Talmud. It is not to be analyzed. It stands as an exemplar for living. It communicates fervor, joy, and the satisfaction of the spiritual life. The tale was often told at a Rebbe's court for the pleasure and instruction of his disciples. Presented by a master storyteller like Wiesel, Hasidic tales are charming in the literal sense of the word.

Souls on Fire: Portraits and Legends of Hasidic Masters developed out of a series of lectures on Hasidism that Wiesel delivered at the Sorbonne in Paris and at The Young Men's Hebrew Association on 92nd Street in New York City. The book is a collection of deliberations on the lives, times, and legends of a succession of great and famous Hasidic rabbis. Wiesel naturally begins with the founder of Hasidism, Israel Baal Shem Tov, and proceeds to discuss the Baal Shem Tov's disciples and long line of successors in Eastern Europe from 1700 to the mid-nineteenth century. In *Souls on Fire,* Wiesel shows general readers what Hasidism has accomplished and, by implication, is still accomplishing today despite the death of so many Hasids in the Holocaust and the transplanting of Hasidic communities to North America and Israel. Hasidic rebbes are storytellers and tellers of parables; so is Wiesel. He admires the way the early Hasidic masters served God and humankind with wisdom, joy, laughter, and love.

Four Hasidic Masters and Their Struggle against Melancholy developed out of Wiesel's love for Hasidic stories and his engagement to lecture on Old World Hasidic tales at the University of Notre Dame. It tells the story of four disciples of the Baal Shem Tov, the founder of Hasidism: Pinhas of Koretz, The seer of Lublin, Barukh of Medzebozh, and Naphtali of Ropshitz. These are lesser known figures in the history of Hasidism, and their lives are shrouded in mystery. The stories are full of the wisdom of the rabbinical sages whose greatness and holiness stem not from unworldliness, but from their common humanity.

Somewhere a Master includes the master rebbes of *Four Hasidic Masters* and adds the legends about four more: Aharon of Karlin, Wolfe of Zbarazh, Moshe-Leib of Sassov, and Meir of Premishlan. Along with the earlier tales, they convey a lost world of a people who found a direct way to God through the simple act of living.

Bible Studies

Orthodox Jews know that the people of the Bible are their ancestors. The Great Book is not only the record of individual lives, it is the record of Jewish life: the original genealogy. In *Messengers of God: Bible Portraits and Legends,* Wiesel presents in very accessible language the legends surrounding the patriarchs and matriarchs as they are discussed, illuminated, and debated in Midrashic literature, that is, the interpretations of Scripture by the rabbis of the Talmud. Wiesel's main subjects are Adam, Cain and Abel, Abraham and the sacrifice of Isaac, Jacob and the Angel, Joseph, and Moses. All the stories are from the Pentateuch. None of the Matriarchs are foregrounded although, of course, they appear.

In *Five Biblical Portraits,* Wiesel continues the talmudic roll call of Patriarchs and Prophets to include Joshua, Elijah, Saul, Jeremiah, and Jonah.

Finally, in *Sages and Dreamers,* Wiesel combines his interest in the Bible, the Talmud, and Hasidic literature into a single volume, again a most readable and enjoyable lesson in Judaica. In "Part One," women are more prominent than in previous studies. Wiesel studies Noah, Jephthah and his Daughter, Ruth, Solomon, Ezekiel, Daniel, Ezra and Nehemiah, and Esther. Surprisingly, David does not get a chapter of his own, although, of course, he figures in the section on his father, Solomon.

"Part Two" discusses the lives of the great talmudic rabbis from before the destruction of the Temple in Jerusalem in 70 A.D., through the great war with Rome that ended in 135 A.D., and up to the middle of the third century A.D.

In "Part Three," Wiesel returns to what seems to be his favorite subjects for storytelling: Hasidic masters. Six more are visited; their wisdom and their woes delineated; and, as with *Souls on Fire, Four Hasidic Masters,* and *Somewhere a Master,* they are introduced by the storyteller to a large new audience of readers of English.

PLAYS

Elie Wiesel has written two full-length plays, *Zalmen, or the Madness of God* (1968c) and *The Trial of God as It Was Held on February 25, 1649, in Shamgorod* (1979). *Zalmen, or the Madness of God* treats anti-Semitism in the Soviet Union in the post–World War II period. The time is the late 1950s. The place is a synagogue in a small Russian town, during the post-Stalin thaw, where political repression has been somewhat relaxed, but the legacy of fear and intimidation endures. Zalmen is the beadle of the synagogue and the narrator/storyteller of the play. He is the point-of-view character in the drama and Wiesel's spokesperson.

A traveling troupe of foreign actors has come to the town. Four Jews in the troupe plan to attend Yom Kippur services in the synagogue. Government officials warn that no one is to complain about lack of religious freedom. Zalmen entreats the rabbi to make a protest; it would be madness, but one has to be mad sometimes to be human. Madness is a tiny part of "the fragile dimension of human hope that Wiesel sees" (Berenbaum 1979, 105). The rabbi speaks out, and the inspector, the Commissar of Jewish Affairs in the Ministry of Culture, comes to the synagogue to investigate the embarrassing incident. The heroic rabbi does not defend his seemingly rash action. Some of the congregation manage to deflect punishment from the rabbi by assuring the power structure that he is an eccentric and that there will be no consequences from his foolish act of rebellion.

In the end, because the rabbi's young grandson understands what his grandfather has done, the boy will grow up to be a dissenter, a Jew who will place love of his religion over the dictates of a controlling, atheistic government. Because God works in a different time frame, this is ultimately the rabbi's and Judaism's victory. The atheistic government will turn to dust while God and the Jews march on.

Yet the play seems to imply that Wiesel thinks God may be mad (Cargas 1990, 155). If that should be the case, it would seem to be best for human beings to join God in the engulfing whirlwind of faith and mysticism, perhaps the nearest state to madness that otherwise rational people can arrive at. The rabbi, egged on by the lowly beadle, did a mad thing, and in so doing pleased God very much.

The Trial of God as It Was Held on February 25, 1649, in Shamgorod is set in the Ukraine shortly after the most terrible event in Jewish European history, the rising in 1648 of Bogdan Chmielnicki, a Ukrainian Cossack leader, who led the massacre of hundreds of thousands of Jews in Poland and Ukraine. He is said to have destroyed more than seven hundred Jewish communities. Today, ironically, Ukrainians regard him as a national hero because he defeated the Poles in battle. The horror of the Chmielnicki assault shocked the Jewish world as nothing had since the destruction of the temple and the expulsion from Judea by the Romans.

In the drama, the time of the year is just prior to Purim, a joyous holiday that celebrates the deliverance of the Jews of Persia from a persecutor as depicted in the Jewish Bible's Book of Esther. It is a carnival time, when dressing in costumes, playacting, clowning, and madcap behavior are permitted.

Three Jewish minstrels have come to an inn hoping to perform for the holiday. They order drinks for which they cannot pay. But the only Jewish survivors of the great Chmielnicki pogrom are the innkeeper, Berish, a giant of a man, and his young daughter, Hanna, who seems to have been driven mad by sexual assault in the attack. The poor minstrels offer to put on a play to pay for their drinks. Berish, angry, does not want an amusing play, but rather a mock trial of God, in which he will serve as a prosecutor. From Berish, we learn that he witnessed the murder of his wife, and that he was forced to witness the gang rape of Hanna by the Cossacks. He indicts God for infidelity to the Jewish people.

Before the trial can begin, a Russian Orthodox priest comes into the inn and warns the Jews of another impending assault. He is willing to give them safety if they will convert to Christianity. The inn maid, Maria, a kind Christian, suggests that the Jews go through a sham ritual to save themselves. Sounding like Wiesel, Maria says: "My God does not persecute me. Yours does nothing else. Why not play a trick on Him? Why not turn your back on Him for a day or a week? Just to teach Him a Lesson!" (48). She is sure that the Jewish God will forgive them. But could they forgive themselves?

The trial commences: the minstrels are the court, and Maria is the witness. God is charged with indifference and even cruelty. Sam, a stranger, enters and he offers to defend God. He turns out to be Satan, when he laughs and raises his hand in a signal. Then, as the curtain falls, the roar of an oncoming murderous crowd is heard through an open door.

Clearly, Wiesel is again addressing the question of theodicy: How can we believe in a just and merciful God, if God allows terrible events such as the Holocaust to happen? The play is both tragedy and farce, a Theater of the Absurd happening that numbs the audience with its audacity and its intensity. This powerful, brilliant, and bitter play comes perilously close to mocking or denying God, yet it is not blasphemy. Belief is unshaken. But Wiesel perhaps finally decided that as in Samuel Beckett's *Waiting for Godot,* God, alas, is just not interested.

Bibliography

WORKS BY ELIE WIESEL

(All are English language editions)

NOVELS

1960. *Night*. Translated from the French by Stella Rodway. New York: Hill and Wang. Reprint, New York: Bantam, 1982.

1961. *Dawn*. Translated from the French by Frances Frenaye. New York: Hill and Wang.

1962. *The Accident*. Translated from the French by Anne Borchardt. New York: Hill and Wang.

1964. *The Town beyond the Wall*. Translated from the French by Stephen Becker. New York: Atheneum.

1966a. *The Gates of the Forest*. Translated from the French by Frances Frenaye. New York: Holt, Rinehart and Winston. Reprint, New York: Schocken, 1982.

1970a. *A Beggar in Jerusalem*. Translated from the French by Lily Edelman and Elie Wiesel. New York: Random House. Reprint, New York: Schocken, 1985.

1973. *The Oath*. Translated from the French by Marion Wiesel. New York: Random House.

1981b. *The Testament*. Translated from the French by Marion Wiesel. New York: Summit Books.

1985. *The Fifth Son*. Translated from the French by Marion Wiesel. New York: Summit.

1988. *Twilight*. Translated from the French by Marion Wiesel. New York: Summit.

1992. *The Forgotten*. Translated from the French by Stephen Becker. New York: Summit.

2002. *The Judges: A Novel*. Translated from the French by Geoffrey Strachan. New York: Knopf.

AUTOBIOGRAPHY

1995. *All Rivers Run to the Sea*. Translated from the French by Jon Rothschild. New York: Knopf.

1999. *And The Sea Is Never Full*. Translated from the French by Marion Wiesel. New York: Knopf.

ESSAYS

1966. *The Jews of Silence: A Personal Report on Soviet Jewry*. Translated from the Hebrew by Neal Kozodoy. New York: Holt, Rinehart and Winston.

1968b. *Legends of Our Time*. Translated from the French by Steven Donadio. New York: Holt, Rinehart and Winston; New York: Schocken, 1982.

1970b. *One Generation After*. Translated from the French by Lily Edelman and Elie Wiesel. New York: Random House; New York: Schocken, 1982.

1978b. *A Jew Today*. Translated from the French by Marion Wiesel. New York: Random House,.

1990. *From the Kingdom of Memory: Reminiscences*. New York: Summit.

HASIDIC AND BIBLICAL STUDIES

1972b. *Souls on Fire: Portraits and Legends of Hasidic Masters*. Translated from the French by Marion Wiesel. New York: Random House.

1976. *Messengers of God: Biblical Portraits and Legends*. Translated from the French by Marion Wiesel. New York: Random House.

1978a. *Four Hasidic Masters and Their Struggle against Melancholy*. South Bend, Ind.: University of Notre Dame Press.

1980. *Images From the Bible*. Woodstock, N.Y.: Overlook.

1981a. *Five Biblical Portraits*. South Bend, Ind.: University of Notre Dame Press.

1982. *Somewhere a Master: Further Tales of the Hasidic Masters*. Translated from the French by Marion Wiesel. New York: Summit.

1983. *The Golem*. Translated from the French by Anne Borchardt. New York: Summit.

1991. *Sages and Dreamers*. Translated from the French by Marion Wiesel. New York: Summit.

PLAYS

1968c. *Zalmen, or the Madness of God*. Translated by Nathan Edelman and adapted for the stage by Marion Wiesel. New York: Random House. Reprint, 1974.
1979. *The Trial of God as It Was Held on February 25, 1649, in Shamgorod*. Translated by Marion Wiesel. New York: Random House.

SELECTED WORKS ABOUT ELIE WIESEL

BIOGRAPHIES

Estess, Ted E. 1980. *Elie Wiesel*. New York: Ungar.
Fine, Ellen S. 1982. *Legacy of Night: The Literary Universe of Elie Wiesel*. Albany: State University of New York Press.
Stern, Ellen Norman. 1982. *Elie Wiesel: Witness for Life*. New York: Ktav.
Walker, Graham B. Jr. 1988. *Elie Wiesel. A Challenge to Theology*. Jefferson, N.C.: McFarland.

CRITICISM AND REVIEWS

Night

Abrahamson, Irving. 1985. "Introductory Essay." In *Against Silence: The Voice and Vision of Elie Wiesel*. Vol. I. Selected and edited by Irving Abrahamson: 7–83. New York: Holocaust Library.
Alvarez, A. 1964. "The Literature of the Holocaust." *Commentary*, November, 65–68.
Berenbaum, Michael. 1979. *The Vision of the Void: Theological Reflections on the Works of Elie Wiesel*. Middletown, Conn.: Wesleyan University Press.
Brown, Robert McAfee. 1983. *Elie Wiesel: Messenger to All Humanity*. South Bend, Ind.: University of Notre Dame Press.
Davis, Colin. 1994. *Elie Wiesel's Secretive Texts*. Gainesville: University Press of Florida.
Hager, Wesley H. 1961. "Beyond Tears and Anger." *Christian Century*, 18 January, 84.
Hamaoui, Lea. 1990. "Historical Horror and the Shape of *Night*." In *Elie Wiesel: Between Memory and Hope*, ed. Carol Rittner, 120–29. New York: New York University Press.
Ivry, Itzhak. 1960. "Memory of Torment." *Saturday Review*, 17 December, 22–23.

Dawn

Berenbaum, Michael. 1979. *The Vision of the Void: Theological Reflections on the Works of Elie Wiesel*. Middletown, Conn.: Wesleyan University Press.

Fine, Ellen S. 1982. *Legacy of Night: The Literary Universe of Elie Wiesel*. Albany: State University of New York Press.

Mitgang, Herbert. 1961. "An Eye for an Eye." *New York Times Book Review*, 16 July, 23.

The Accident

Brown, Robert McAfee. 1983. *Elie Wiesel: Messenger to All Humanity*. South Bend, Ind.: University of Notre Dame Press.

Estess, Ted E. 1980. *Elie Wiesel*. New York: Ungar.

Fine, Ellen S. 1982. *Legacy of Night: The Literary Universe of Elie Wiesel*. Albany: State University of New York Press.

Leddy, Mary Jo. 1990. "Between Destruction and Creation." In *Elie Wiesel: Between Memory and Hope*, ed. Carol Rittner, 42–49. New York: New York University Press.

Mitgang. Herbert. 1963. "Suspended between Life and Death." *New York Times Book Review*, 15 April, 36.

Pine, John C. 1962. "*The Accident*." *Library Journal* 1 (March): 996.

Roth, John K. 1990. "Elie Wiesel's Challenge to Christianity." In *Elie Wiesel: Between Memory and Hope*, ed. Carol Rittner, 78–96. New York: New York University Press.

The Town beyond the Wall

Berenbaum, Michael. 1979. *The Vision of the Void: Theological Reflections on the Works of Elie Wiesel*. Middletown, Conn.: Wesleyan University Press.

Estess, Ted E. 1980. *Elie Wiesel*. New York: Ungar.

Friedman, Joseph J. 1964. "The Shame of Survival." *Saturday Review*, 25 July, 26.

Friedman, Maurice. 1978. "Eli Wiesel: The Job of Auschwitz." In *Responses to Elie Wiesel: Critical Essays by Major Jewish and Christian Scholars*, ed. Harry James Cargas, 205–30. New York: Persea.

Stern, Daniel. 1964. "Suicide, Madness, or God." *New York Times Book Review*, 5 July, 14.

The Gates of the Forest

Berenbaum, Michael. 1979. *The Vision of the Void: Theological Reflections on the Works of Elie Wiesel*. Middletown, Conn.: Wesleyan University Press.

Daiches, David. 1965. "After Such Knowledge . . . " *Commentary*, December, 105–10.

Davis, Colin. 1994. *Elie Wiesel's Secretive Texts*. Gainesville: University Press of Florida.

Elman, Richard M. 1966. "Betrayed into Living." *New York Times Book Review*, 18 July, 5.

Fine, Ellen S. 1982. *Legacy of Night: The Literary Universe of Elie Wiesel*. Albany: State University of New York Press.

Halpern, Irving. 1978. "From *Night* to *The Gates of the Forest:* The Novels of Elie Wiesel." In *Responses to Elie Wiesel: Critical Essays by Major Jewish and Christian Scholars*, ed. Harry James Cargas, 45–82. New York: Persea.

Stern, Daniel. 1990. "Elie Wiesel: A Thirty-Year Dialogue between Hope and Despair." In *Elie Wiesel: Between Memory and Hope*, ed. Carol Rittner, 10–28. New York: New York University Press.

Wain, John. 1966. "The Insult and Injured." *New York Review of Books*, 28 July, 22–23.

A Beggar in Jerusalem

Des Pres, Terrence. 1978. "The Authority of Silence in Elie Wiesel's Art." In *Confronting the Holocaust: The Impact of Elie Wiesel*, ed. Alvin H. Rosenfeld and Irving Greenberg, 49–57. Bloomington: Indiana University Press.

Estess, Ted E. 1980. *Elie Wiesel*. New York: Ungar.

Fine, Ellen S. 1982. *Legacy of Night: The Literary Universe of Elie Wiesel*. Albany: State University of New York Press.

Friedman, Maurice. 1978. "Elie Wiesel: The Job of Auschwitz." In *Responses to Elie Wiesel: Critical Essays by Major Jewish and Christian Scholars*, ed. Harry James Cargas, 205–30. New York: Persea.

Kahn, Lothar. 1990. "Elie Wiesel: Neo-Hasidism." In *Elie Wiesel: Between Memory and Hope*, ed. Carol Rittner, 102–14. New York: New York University Press.

Langer, Lawrence L. 1978. "The Divided Voice: Elie Wiesel and the Challenge of the Holocaust." In *Confronting the Holocaust: The Impact of Elie Wiesel*, ed. Alvin H. Rosenfeld and Irving Greenberg, 31–48. Bloomington: Indiana University Press.

Leviant, Curt. 1970. "Elie Wiesel: A Soul on Fire." *Saturday Review*, 31 January, 25–28.

Pritchett, V. S. 1970. "Ghosts." *New York Review of Books*, 7 May, 12.

Sperber, Manes. 1970. "A Beggar in Jerusalem." *New York Times Book Review*, 25 January, 1, 34.

The Oath

Berenbaum, Michael. 1979. *The Vision of the Void: Theological Reflections on the Works of Elie Wiesel*. Middletown, Conn.: Wesleyan University Press.

Davis, Colin. 1994. *Elie Wiesel's Secretive Texts*. Gainesville: University Press of Florida.

Estess, Ted E. 1980. *Elie Wiesel*. New York: Ungar.

Fine, Ellen S. 1982. *Legacy of Night: The Literary Universe of Elie Wiesel*. Albany: State University of New York Press.

Friedman, Alan. 1973. "Chronicle of a Pogrom: *The Oath*." *New York Times Book Review*, 18 November, 5.

Lamont, Rosette C. 1990. "Elie Wiesel's Poetics of Madness." In *Elie Wiesel: Between Memory and Hope*, ed. Carol Rittner, 130–52. New York: New York University Press.

Roth, John K. 1978. "Telling a Tale That Cannot Be Told: Reflections on the Authorship of Elie Wiesel." In *Confronting the Holocaust: The Impact of Elie Wiesel*, ed. Alvin H. Rosenfeld and Irving Greenberg, 49–79. Bloomington: Indiana University Press.

Stern, Ellen Norman. 1982. *Elie Wiesel: Witness for Life*. New York: Ktav.

Wood, Michael. 1974. "Victims of Survival." *New York Review of Books*, 7 February, 11–12.

The Testament, The Fifth Son, Twilight, The Forgotten, The Judges

Brown, Robert McAfee. 1981. "The Power of the Tale." *Christian Century*, 3–10 June, 649–52.

———. 1985. "Elie Wiesel's *The Fifth Son*." *Christian Century*, 15 May, 497–99.

Busch, Frederick. 1992. "An Endangered Witness." *New York Times Book Review*, 19 April, 8.

Chamberlain, Lesley. 1988. "Tortures of Man and God." *Times Literary Supplement*, 18 November, 1284.

Davis, Colin. 1994. *Elie Wiesel's Secretive Texts*. Gainesville: University Press of Florida.

Morton, Frederic. 1998. "Execution as an Act of Intimacy." *New York Times Book Review*, 24 March, 9.

Moss, Stanley. 1988. "Adam and Cain in the Madhouse." *New York Times Book Review*, 10 July, 12.

Rosen, Jonathan. 2002. "Five Passengers and a Judge with Murder on His Mind." *New York Times*, 25 October, 41.

Shack, Neville. 1986. "Legacy of Anguish." *Times Literary Supplement*, 6 June, 622.

Stern, Daniel. 1990. "Elie Wiesel: A Thirty-Year Dialogue between Hope and Despair." In *Elie Wiesel: Between Memory and Hope*, ed. Carol Rittner, 10–28. New York: New York University Press.

Sullivan, Patrick. 2002. "The Judges." *Library Journal* 1 (June): 198.

Taylor, Paul. 1988. "An Obsessive Quest of Memory and Madness." London *Times*, 13 November, G6.

SELECTED NONFICTION

Berenbaum, Michael. 1979. *The Vision of the Void: Theological Reflections on the Works of Elie Wiesel*. Middletown, Conn.: Wesleyan University Press.

AUTOBIOGRAPHY, BIBLICAL STUDIES AND HASIDIC STORIES, AND PLAYS

Berenbaum, Michael. 1979. *The Vision of the Void: Theological Reflections on the Works of Elie Wiesel*. Middletown, Conn.: Wesleyan University Press.

Cargas, Harry James. 1990. "Drama Reflecting Madness." In *Elie Wiesel: Between Memory and Hope*, ed. Carol Rittner, 153–62. New York: New York University Press.

OTHER SECONDARY SOURCES

Brown, Robert McAfee. 1983. *Elie Wiesel: Messenger to All Humanity*. South Bend, Ind.: University of Notre Dame Press.

Cargas, Harry James. 1976. *Conversations with Elie Wiesel*. South Bend, Ind.: Justice Books. Revised edition, 1992.

———. 1978. *Responses to Elie Wiesel: Critical Essays by Major Jewish and Christian Scholars*. New York: Persea.

Cheron, Michaël de Saint. 1990. *Evil and Exile: Elie Wiesel*. Translated by Jon Rothschild and Jody Gladding. South Bend, Ind.: University of Notre Dame Press.

Ezrahi, Sidra DeKoven. 1980. *By Words Alone*. Chicago: University of Chicago Press.

Roth, John K. 1979. *A Consuming Fire: Encounters with Elie Wiesel and the Holocaust*. Atlanta: John Knox.

Sibelman, Simon P. 1995. *Silence in the Novels of Eli Wiesel*. New York: Palgrave Macmillan.

Young, James E. 1998. *Writing and Rewriting the Holocaust: Narrative and the Consequences of Interpretation*. Bloomington: Indiana University Press.

Index

About the Author

SANFORD STERNLICHT teaches in Syracuse University's English Department and Judaic Studies Program. He is the author of *Chaim Potok: A Critical Companion* (Greenwood 2000). He also frequently writes on drama and Irish literature, including contributions to *Modern Irish Writers: A Bio-Critical Sourcebook* (Greenwood 1997).